ALGEBRA

Authors: Myrl Shireman and Don Blattner
Editor: Mary Dieterich
Proofreaders: April Albert and Margaret Brown

COPYRIGHT © 2018 Mark Twain Media, Inc.

ISBN 978-1-62223-701-2

Printing No. CD-405024

Mark Twain Media, Inc., Publishers
Distributed by Carson-Dellosa Publishing LLC

Visit us at www.carsondellosa.com

Table of Contents

Table of Contents (cont.)

Introduction

Algebra is increasingly becoming a required course in the curriculum of many schools. Algebra is also the keystone course students need as they begin developing the mathematics skills needed in today's world. However, many students enrolled in today's algebra classes will not succeed without frequent opportunities to practice the skills required for success in algebra. The skills emphasized in this book are those that are basic to understanding the major concepts taught in Algebra I.

Each skill introduced is followed by examples, the opportunity to practice the skill, and a short quiz over the concept. The emphasis of the material in each lesson is on understanding and using the basic concept in the lesson rather than giving broad coverage. This format is followed because the success of many students depends on ample explanation followed by practice lessons that allow the student to gain confidence in using the skills.

This book may be used by parents or teachers as a primer prior to introducing the basic concepts that will be needed in algebra. It is also designed as a supplement to be used by classroom teachers to provide extra practice on some of the key skills taught in Algebra I.

Name: _____   Date: _____

Positive and Negative Numbers
ADDING POSITIVE AND NEGATIVE NUMBERS

Understanding how positive and negative numbers are used in addition, subtraction, multiplication, and division is important in the study of algebra. In addition problems, the numbers may all be positive, all negative, or include both positive and negative numbers.

> **A.** To add numbers with like signs, add the numbers and place the sign in front of the sum.
>
> **B.** To add numbers with unlike signs, subtract the numbers and place the sign of the larger number in front of the sum.

Examples:

	A		A		B		B
	1) +8	2)	-8	3)	-8	4)	+8
	+ +3		+ -3		+ +3		+ -3
	+11		-11		-5		+5

Directions: Refer to A and B above and solve the following problems. Place the letter A or B above each problem to indicate the rule used to solve the problem. The first one is completed.

1. (A)
+4
+ +2
+6

2. -7
+ -8

3. -9
+ +7

4. -23
+ -45

5. -67
+ +78

6. +89
+ +67

7. +9 and -6 = _____

8. +45 and -67 = _____

9. +34 and -25 = _____

10. -78 and -65 = _____

11. +145 and +231 = _____

12. -14 and +100 = _____

> **When adding three or more numbers, first add the numbers with like signs and then add the numbers with different signs.**

Examples: Adding the numbers (-8) + (-7) + (+9)
    Add: -8 + -7 = -15 Then add: (-15) + (+9) = -6

    Adding the numbers (+12) + (-16) + (-12) + (- 7)
    Add: (-16) + (-12) + (-7) = -35 Then add: (-35) + (+12) = -23

Directions: Solve the following problems.

13. -3
-9
+5
+ -4

14. +8
-18
-24
+ +12

15. -23
-18
+9
+ - 35

16. +34
-89
-78
+ +4

17. -78
+12
-45
+ +10

18. -6
-23
-7
+ -3

Name: _____ Date: _____

SUBTRACTING POSITIVE AND NEGATIVE NUMBERS

Subtraction: In learning about subtracting positive and negative numbers, it is important to review the terms **minuend**, **subtrahend,** and **difference**.

Example: Subtract 2 from 8

$$
\begin{array}{rcl}
+8 & = & \text{minuend} \\
-\ +2 & = & \text{subtrahend} \\
\hline
+6 & = & \text{difference}
\end{array}
$$

An important rule to remember in subtraction is that the subtrahend and difference when added should equal the minuend. In the example above, 2 + 6 = 8

Subtraction of positive and negative numbers: To subtract using positive and negative numbers you must *change the sign* of the subtrahend and add.

Example: To subtract

$$
\begin{array}{l}
+8 \\
-\ +2
\end{array}
\quad \text{change the sign of the subtrahend} \quad
\begin{array}{l}
+8 \\
+\ -2 \\
\hline
+6
\end{array}
\quad \text{and add.}
$$

Check: Adding the original subtrahend (+2) to the difference (+6) equals +8 (the minuend).

Example: To subtract

$$
\begin{array}{l}
-8 \\
-\ +2
\end{array}
\quad \text{change the sign of the subtrahend} \quad
\begin{array}{l}
-8 \\
+\ -2 \\
\hline
-10
\end{array}
\quad \text{and add.}
$$

Check: Adding the subtrahend (+2) to the difference (-10) equals -8 (the minuend).

Directions: Solve the following problems. Change the sign of the subtrahend in "A" and write the new subtrahend in "B." Find the difference and record the difference beneath the line in "B." The first one has been completed.

1.
A	B
+ 9	+9
- - 5	+ +5
	+14

2.
A	B
-12	-12
- +14	+ ___

3.
A	B
-89	-89
- +18	+ ___

4.
A	B
+15	+15
- - 23	+ ___

Check 1) +14 + -5 = +9   **Check 2)** - _____ + _____ = - _____

Check 3) - _____ + _____ = - _____   **Check 4)** + _____ + _____ = + _____

5. 8 - (-5) = _____   **6.** -23 - (+5) - (+7) = _____   **7.** (-16) - (-7) = _____

8. What number must be added to the subtrahend to get the minuend? _____

Name: _____ Date: _____

Quiz I: Addition and Subtraction
With Positive and Negative Numbers

1. Under column A, write the addition problem (+90) + (-123) in column form in the space below, and solve the problem. Then, under column B, write the terms **addend** and **sum** on the blanks to correctly identify each.

                              A   **B**

                                        _____

                            _____   _____

                                        _____

Directions: Solve the following **addition** problems.

2.	+45	**3.**	-64	**4.**	+124	**5.**	+43	**6.**	-189	**7.**	-489
	+ +34		+ +9		+ -35		+ +56		+ +278		+ -34

8. Under column A, write the subtraction problem (+90) - (-123) in column form in the space below, and solve the problem. Then, under column B, write the terms **subtrahend**, **difference**, and **minuend** on the blanks to correctly identify each.

                              A   **B**

                                        _____

                            _____   _____

                                        _____

Directions: Solve the following **subtraction** problems.

9.	+45	**10.**	-64	**11.**	+124	**12.**	-278	**13.**	+239	**14.**	- 489
	- +34		- +9		- -35		- +189		- -104		- -34

Directions: Match the term in Column A with the definition in Column B.

Column A	**Column B**
_____ **15.** minuend	**A.** The result of an addition
_____ **16.** subtrahend	**B.** A number to be added
_____ **17.** difference	**C.** The first number in a subtraction problem
_____ **18.** addend	**D.** The answer in a subtraction problem
_____ **19.** sum	**E.** The number to be subtracted from another

Name: _____ Date: _____

  MULTIPLICATION WITH POSITIVE AND NEGATIVE NUMBERS

> When multiplying two numbers with *unlike* signs, multiply as usual and place a *negative* sign in front of the *product*.

     Example: (+8) x (-6) = -48 or $\begin{array}{r} +8 \\ \times\ -6 \\ \hline -48 \end{array}$

> When multiplying two numbers with *like* signs, multiply as usual and place a *positive* sign in front of the *product*.

    Example: (-8) x (-6) = +48 or $\begin{array}{r} -8 \\ \times\ -6 \\ \hline +48 \end{array}$ *Example:* (+8) x (+6) = +48 or $\begin{array}{r} +8 \\ \times\ +6 \\ \hline +48 \end{array}$

Directions: Multiply the following problems. Place the correct sign in front of each product. In the blanks by each problem, state the rule used to determine the sign for the product: **like signs rule** or **unlike signs rule**.

1. $\begin{array}{r} +8 \\ \times\ +4 \\ \hline \end{array}$ _____

2. $\begin{array}{r} -80 \\ \times\ +6 \\ \hline \end{array}$ _____

3. $\begin{array}{r} -7 \\ \times\ +5 \\ \hline \end{array}$ _____

4. $\begin{array}{r} -24 \\ \times\ -13 \\ \hline \end{array}$ _____

> When multiplying three or more numbers, multiply from left to right. The sign of the product will be determined by the last two numbers multiplied.

    Example: multiply (+8) x (-6) x (-4) = +192
            Step 1: (+8) x (-6) = -48   (plus x minus = minus)
            Step 2: (-48) x (-4) = +192 (minus x minus = plus)

Directions: Multiply the following problems. Place the correct sign in front of each answer. Indicate the steps followed to get the answer.

5. (-6) x (-2) x (+7) =   Step 1: ____ x ____ = _____   Step 2: ____ x ____ = _____

6. (+8) x (-5) x (-9) =   Step 1: ____ x ____ = _____   Step 2: ____ x ____ = _____

7. (-7) x (-8) x (-10) =   Step 1: ____ x ____ = _____   Step 2: ____ x ____ = _____

8. (+7) x (+4) x (-2) =   Step 1: ____ x ____ = _____   Step 2: ____ x ____ = _____

Name: _____   Date: _____

 DIVISION WITH POSITIVE AND NEGATIVE NUMBERS

> **When dividing numbers with *like* signs, find the quotient and place the positive sign in front of the quotient.**

> *Example:* $\frac{12}{6}$ = +12 ÷ +6 = +2 (dividing numbers with **like** signs)

> *Example:* $\frac{-12}{-6}$ = -12 ÷ -6 = +2 (dividing numbers with **like** signs)

> **When dividing numbers with *unlike* signs, find the quotient and place the negative sign in front of the quotient.**

> *Example:* $\frac{12}{-6}$ = +12 ÷ -6 = -2 (dividing numbers with **unlike** signs)

> *Example:* $\frac{-12}{6}$ = -12 ÷ +6 = -2 (dividing numbers with **unlike** signs)

Directions: Solve the following division problems using positive and negative numbers. Refer to the examples and fill in the blanks. Place the correct sign before the quotient. Write the rule for determining the sign of the quotient on the blank below each problem: **like signs rule** or **unlike signs rule**.

1. $+\frac{18}{3}$ = ____ ÷ ____ = ____   _____

2. $\frac{-18}{3}$ = ____ ÷ ____ = ____   _____

3. $\frac{-18}{-3}$ = ____ ÷ ____ = ____   _____

4. $\frac{18}{-3}$ = ____ ÷ ____ = ____   _____

Directions: Solve the following problems. Write the quotient with the correct sign on the blank.

5. $\frac{256}{2}$ = _____

6. $\frac{625}{25}$ = _____

7. $\frac{-338}{13}$ = _____

8. $\frac{784}{14}$ = _____

Name: _____ Date: _____

Quiz II: Multiplication and Division With Positive and Negative Numbers

Directions: Solve the following multiplication problems using positive and negative numbers.

1. (+23) x (-14) = _____

2. (-13) x (-9) = _____

3. (-123) x (+44) = _____

4. (+67) x (+5) x (+45) x (+12) = _____

5. (- 34) x (+7) x (+78) = _____

6. (-3) x (+41) x (+2) = _____

Directions: Solve and discover the pattern in the following multiplication problems.

7. (-2) x (-5) = _____

8. (-6) x (-9) x (-2) = _____

9. (-12) x (-10) x (-3) x (-5) = _____

10. (-10) x (-11) x (-9) x (-6) x (-3) = _____

11. (-7) x (-4) x (-9) x (-10) x (-8) x (-9) = _____

12. (-2) x (-4) x (-9) x (-1) x (-7) x (-6) x (-2) = _____

Directions: Each of the following statements has an error. Find the error and write a corrected statement on the blank below each statement.

13. When 2, 4, 6, or 8 numbers are multiplied, the product will have a negative sign.

_____

14. When 1, 3, 5, or 7 numbers are multiplied, the product will have a positive sign.

_____

Directions: Solve the following division problems using positive and negative numbers.

15. (+12) ÷ (-2) = _____

16. (+52) ÷ (+13) = _____

17. (-88) ÷ (-11) = _____

18. (-125) ÷ (+5) = _____

19. (-228) ÷ (-3) = _____

20. (-96) ÷ (+2) = _____

Directions: Each of the following statements contains an error. Find the error and write the correct answer on the blank below the statement.

21. When dividing two numbers with different signs, the quotient will have the sign of the larger number.

_____

22. When dividing two numbers with the same sign, the quotient will have the opposite sign.

_____

Mathematical Symbols
VARIABLES

In algebra, letters are often used to represent numbers. Although any letter may be used to represent a given number, the letters x and y are used frequently. When letters are used to represent numbers, the letter may be a **constant** or a **variable**. A letter is called a variable when many different numerical values can be assigned to that letter. The variable is often called the **unknown**. A constant is a number or letter that represents a fixed number. It does not change.

Example: $8 + x = 12$. In this case, only one numerical value may be assigned to the letter x. $4, \frac{8}{2}, 3\frac{3}{3}, \frac{4}{1}$ are numerals that might replace the letter x, but the numerical value of each of the numerals is 4. In this example the letter x is a constant.

Example: $8 + x = $ ___. Any numerical value may be assigned to the letter x. In this example, the letter x is a variable.

In learning about constants and variables, it is important to review some of the symbols that will be used in the lessons that follow.

EQUAL, LESS THAN, GREATER THAN

A sentence with an **equal sign** (=) is an equation. An **equation** means that the value of the number or numbers on the left of the equal sign is equal to the value of the number or numbers on the right.

Examples: $15 = 15$ $15 = 10 + 5$ $15 = 10 + 10 - 5$
$8 + x = 12$ x must equal 4

The symbol $<$ means **less than.** If a problem states that x is less than y, then the problem is written $x < y$. You can easily remember which number is smaller because the symbol always points to the smaller number.

Examples: $14 < 15$ $13 < 10 + 5$ $11 < 8 + 8 - 3$
$8 + x < 12$ (x cannot be +4 or greater)

The symbol $>$ means **greater than.** If a problem states that x is greater than y, then the problem is written $x > y$. You can easily remember which number is smaller because the symbol always points to the smaller number.

Examples: $16 > 15$ $18 > 5 + 4 + 3$ $14 > 7 + 9 - 3$
$8 + x > 12$ (x must be greater than +4)

Name: _____ Date: _____

MORE MATHEMATICAL SYMBOLS

Here are other mathematical symbols you will be using in algebra. You are already familiar with some of them.

($\leq$) means "is less than or equal to"	$8 + x \leq 12$ x must be +4 or less
($\geq$) means "is greater than or equal to"	$8 + x \geq 12$ x must be +4 or more
(+) means "to find the sum"	$8 + x = 12$
(-) means "to subtract or find the difference"	$8 - x = 6$
($\div$ or /) means "to divide"	$8 \div x = 4$ or $8/x = 4$

(• or a number or variable written next to another number or variable) means "to multiply or find the product" $8 \cdot x = 16$ or $8x = 16$

Directions: Fill in the blanks with the symbols = or < or >.

1. 3 ___ 5   **2.** 7 ___ 3   **3.** 0.3 ___ 1   **4.** 12 ___ 1.00

5. 1.3 ___ 1.33   **6.** 0.19 ___ 1.01   **7.** 0.22 ___ 0.022   **8.** 2.2 ___ 2.02

9. $\frac{1}{2}$ ___ $\frac{2}{3}$ **10.** $\frac{7}{2}$ ___ $\frac{2}{7}$ **11.** $\frac{8}{10}$ ___ 0.8   **12.** $\frac{10}{15}$ ___ $\frac{2}{3}$

13. $\frac{1}{3}$ ___ 0.33   **14.** $2\frac{2}{3}$ ___ 2.57   **15.** $3\frac{2}{5}$ ___ 3.4   **16.** 0.067 ___ 0.67

Directions: a) Solve the following problems and b) circle the correct word.

17. $16 + x = 4$ **a)** $x =$ _____   **b)** x is a (constant/variable).

18. $36 - 7 = y$ **a)** $y =$ _____   **b)** y a (constant/variable).

19. $88 \div x = 8$ **a)** $x =$ _____   **b)** x is a (constant/variable).

20. $20x = 80$ **a)** $x =$ _____   **b)** x is a (constant/variable).

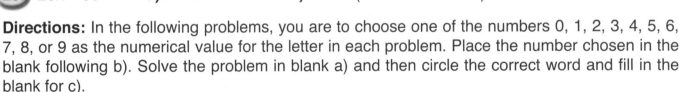

Directions: In the following problems, you are to choose one of the numbers 0, 1, 2, 3, 4, 5, 6, 7, 8, or 9 as the numerical value for the letter in each problem. Place the number chosen in the blank following b). Solve the problem in blank a) and then circle the correct word and fill in the blank for c).

21. $16 + x = ?$ **a)** _____   **b)** $x =$ _____   **c)** x is a (constant/variable) because

_____

22. $36 - y = ?$ **a)** _____   **b)** $y =$ _____   **c)** y is a (constant/variable) because

_____

23. $88 \div x = ?$ **a)** _____   **b)** $x =$ _____   **c)** x is a (constant/variable) because

_____

24. $20x = ?$ **a)** _____   **b)** $x =$ _____   **c)** x is a (constant/ variable) because

_____

Name: _____ Date: _____

 MATH PROBLEMS WITH MORE THAN ONE VARIABLE

Problems often include more than one letter or variable.

Example: $x + y = 4$

In this problem, the letters x and y are both variables. Some of the numerical values that can replace x or y in the problem are 2, 1, 3, 0, 4, $3\frac{1}{2}$, $\frac{1}{2}$, and so forth. The numerical values chosen must equal 4. If $x = 4$ then y must equal 0. If $x = \frac{1}{2}$ then y must equal $3\frac{1}{2}$.

Directions: Solve the following. Choose the answers from the following numbers: -8, -7, -6, -5, -4, -3, -2, -1, 0, +1, +2, +3, +4, +5, +6, +7, +8. Write the answers on the blank following each problem.

1. $x + y = 6$ _____   **2.** $x \div y = 36$ _____

3. $\frac{x}{y} = 36$ _____   **4.** $xy = 25$ _____

5. $x \cdot y = 25$ _____   **6.** $x - y = 3$ _____

There are times when numbers and letters occur in various combinations such as those in the following examples.

$$3x, \ 3x - 1, \ x + 4y, \ \frac{x}{6}, \ \frac{x}{8} + 2y, \text{ and so forth}$$

Example: $3x =$ ___

In this expression, the operation to be performed is multiplication. The 3 is a **constant** and the x is the **variable** or **unknown**. The expression indicates that 3 is to be multiplied times the value assigned to x.

Possible answers: $3 \cdot 1 = 3$; $3 \cdot 2 = 6$; $3 \cdot 3 = 9$; $3 \cdot (-1) = -3$; $3 \cdot (-2) = -6$; $3 \cdot (-3) = -9$

Directions: Solve the following problems.

7. If $x = 5$ then $4x =$ _____   **8.** If $x = 7$ then $4 \cdot x =$ _____

9. If $x = -7$ then $4x =$ _____   **10.** If $y = 5$ then $3y - 1 =$ _____

11. If $y = 6$ then $3y - 1 =$ _____   **12.** If $y = -2$ then $3y - 1 =$ _____

13. If $t = 36$ then $\frac{t}{6} =$ _____   **14.** If $t = -18$ then $\frac{t}{6} =$ _____

15. If $t = -48$ then $t \div 6 =$ _____   **16.** If $x = 24$ and $y = 4$ then $\frac{x}{8} + 2y =$ _____

17. If $x = -144$ and $y = -5$ then $\frac{x}{8} + 2y =$ _____   **18.** If $x = -9$ and $y = -3$ then $x + 4y =$ _____

19. If $x = 46$ and $y = -12$ then $x + 4y =$ _____   **20.** If $b = 4$ and $t = 7$ then $bt - tb =$ _____

WORD PROBLEMS USING VARIABLES

Directions: Circle the correct answers and fill in the blanks to solve the following problems.

1. Emily and two friends wanted to buy a pizza. A small pizza cost $4.50. The next larger pizza cost one dollar more than twice as much as the $4.50 one. They decided to buy the larger pizza. One of them said the algebraic expression to determine the cost could be written as $2x + 1$.

The numeral "2" in the expression is used to mean:

a) twice as much   **b)** $4.50   **c)** one dollar.

2. In solving the problem, the letter "x" in the expression will be replaced by:

a) $1   **b)** $4.50   **c)** 2

3. Place the correct numbers in the expression and find the cost of the pizza.

$2 \cdot$ _____ $+ 1 = \$$ _____

4. Another evening Emily and two friends wanted to buy a pizza. They called another pizza shop and were told that a small pizza cost $4.50. The next larger pizza cost one dollar less than twice as much as the $4.50 one. They decided to buy the larger pizza. The bill was $8.00.

Complete each of the following algebraic expressions and determine which one would give Emily and her friends the correct answer.

a) $2x + 1 = 2 \cdot$ _____ $+ 1 =$ _____   **b)** $3x + 1 = 3 \cdot$ _____ $+ 1 =$ _____

c) $3x - 1 = 3 \cdot$ _____ $- 1 =$ _____   **d)** $2x - 1 = 2 \cdot$ _____ $- 1 =$ _____

5. The algebraic expression that gives the correct answer to the cost of the pizza is

_____ - _____ = $8.00

6. The algebraic expression tells you to take ____ times $ _____ and (add/subtract) $ _____

7. In the blank following each algebraic expression write out in your own words what the expression tells you to do.

a) xy _____   **b)** $\frac{x}{y}$ _____

c) $x + y$ _____   **d)** $x - y$ _____

e) $\frac{x}{y} + ts - 2$ _____

f) $x + \frac{y}{3} + 1$ _____

Name: _____   Date: _____

Quiz III: Mathematical Symbols

Directions: Match the correct definition in Column B with the term or symbol in Column A.

Column A	Column B
_____ **1.** Variable	**A.** Symbol meaning "to divide"
_____ **2.** Constant	**B.** Symbol meaning "equal to"
_____ **3.** =	**C.** Symbol meaning "greater than"
_____ **4.** ≠	**D.** Symbol meaning "does not equal"
_____ **5.** ÷	**E.** Symbol meaning "to find the sum"
_____ **6.** >	**F.** Symbol meaning "equal to or greater than"
_____ **7.** <	**G.** Symbol meaning "to find the difference"
_____ **8.** ≥	**H.** Letter in algebraic expression that may have different values
_____ **9.** ≤	**I.** Variables are to be multiplied
_____ **10.** –	**J.** A number stated in the algebraic expression
_____ **11.** +	**K.** Symbol meaning "equal to or less than"
_____ **12.** xy	**L.** Symbol meaning "less than"

Directions: Write a statement explaining what each of the following algebraic expressions directs you to do.

13. $x = y + 1$ _____

14. $5 \geq x$ _____

15. $\frac{t}{w} - cu$ _____

16. $x + 1 < 5$ _____

17. $x \neq y$ _____

18. $6 + 7 > x$ _____

Name: _____   Date: _____

Understanding Polynomials
DEFINITIONS

A **polynomial** is an algebraic expression of two or more terms. In learning about polynomials, it is important to understand the meaning of the words **number, variable, product, quotient, sum, difference, expression,** and **term.**

- **Number:** Real Numbers include the positive and negative numbers …-5, -4, -3, -2, -1, 0, 1, 2, 3, 4, 5… and numbers that can be expressed as fractions ($\frac{a}{b}$) …$-\frac{1}{4}$, $-\frac{1}{2}$, $-1\frac{1}{2}$, $-1\frac{2}{3}$, $\frac{1}{4}$, $\frac{1}{2}$, $\frac{2}{3}$, $\frac{5}{8}$, $2\frac{3}{4}$, $23\frac{2}{3}$…

- **Variable:** A symbol that may be replaced by one or more numbers. Usually letters of the alphabet are used as variables. In algebra, x and y are often used. A variable may appear alone as x or with some other letter. Often the variable will appear with a number. For example, the number 2 with the variable x becomes $2x$ or 2 multiplied by x. In this case, x is a variable because any number may be substituted for the variable x.

- **Product:** The result of multiplication. For example, in $3 \cdot 6 = 18$, 18 is the product.

- **Quotient:** The result of division. For example, in $\frac{6}{3} = 2$, 2 is the quotient.

- **Sum:** The result of addition. For example, in $6 + 3 = 9$, 9 is the sum.

- **Difference:** The result of subtraction. For example, in $6 - 2 = 4$, 4 is the difference.

- **Expression:** A combination of letters and numbers joined by plus symbols, minus symbols, multiplication symbols, or division symbols.

- **Term:** Parts of an expression separated by plus or minus signs. For example: $4x - 7y$ is a mathematical expression. Both $4x$ and $7y$ are terms.

Place a plus (+) on the blanks before the items below that are **numbers**.

— **1.** x — **2.** 321   — **3.** xy — **4.** $\frac{3}{4}$ — **5.** $56\frac{2}{5}$ — **6.** 24

Place a plus (+) on the blanks before the items below that are **variables**.

— **7.** y — **8.** xy — **9.** $\frac{7}{8}$ — **10.** $\frac{x}{y}$ — **11.** 567   — **12.** b

Place a plus (+) on the blanks before the problems below where a **product** would result.

— **13.** $6 \cdot 7$ — **14.** $5 \cdot x$ — **15.** $8 + 3$ — **16.** $5\frac{6}{3}$ — **17.** $6 \cdot x \cdot y$

Place a plus (+) on the blanks before the problems below where a **quotient** would result.

— **18.** $\frac{2}{3} \cdot \frac{1}{2}$ — **19.** $\frac{a}{b}$ — **20.** $x + y$ — **21.** $\frac{1}{2} \div \frac{2}{3}$ — **22.** $-10 + 5$

Place a plus (+) on the blanks before the problems below where a **sum** would result.

— **23.** $23 + 78$ — **24.** $\frac{3}{4} + \frac{1}{2}$ — **25.** $45x$ — **26.** $2\frac{4}{6}$ — **27.** $7 - 4$

Place a plus (+) on the blanks before the problems below where a **difference** would result.

— **28.** $x - b$ — **29.** $x + b$ — **30.** $56 - 31$ — **31.** $\frac{66}{11}$ — **32.** $72 - (-8)$

Name: _____ Date: _____

TERMS, EXPRESSIONS, AND POLYNOMIALS

A **term** is an expression that may be a number and a variable, a number, a variable, or the product or quotient of numbers and/or variables. **A term represents one number.**

For example: 5, 5a, 5ab, 5a^2b, 5a^2b^2, $\frac{4}{2}$ are all terms that represent one number.

For each term in the example above, let $a = 2$, $b = 3$, and find what number each of the terms represents.

$5 = 5$ $5a = 5 \cdot 2 = 10$ $5ab = 5 \cdot 2 \cdot 3 = 30$ $5a^2b = 5 \cdot 2^2 \cdot 3 = 60$

$5a^2b^2 = 5 \cdot 2^2 \cdot 3^2 = 180$ $\frac{4}{2} = 2$

Directions: Place a plus (+) on the blanks before the items below that are **terms**.

— **1.** 3a — **2.** 34   — **3.** y — **4.** 21 + 6   — **5.** 89 - 23

— **6.** 8ax — **7.** $x + y$ — **8.** 3x - y — **9.** 3/b — **10.** $x + y$/5

In algebra the word **expression** is used frequently. An **expression** consists of one, two, or three terms and represents a **number**. In an expression, the terms are composed of **numbers** and **letters (variables)** together or **numbers** and **letters (variables)** separately. For example: The expression 5a has one term. The expression 5 has one term. The expression 5a + 5 has two terms. The expression 5a - 2b + 5 has three terms.

> When an expression includes terms using both numbers and letters (variables), the expression is called an *algebraic expression*.

Directions: Place a plus (+) on the blanks before the expressions below that have **two or more terms**.

— **11.** xy — **12.** $x + y$ — **13.** 6a - b — **14.** 8$x + \frac{7}{8}$ — **15.** 2xy/2

— **16.** 5z - 2x — **17.** 32 + xy — **18.** 4xy — **19.** s/b — **20.** s/x + 10a

Polynomial refers to an **expression** of one, two, or three **terms**. Polynomials of one term are called **monomials**. Polynomials of two terms are called **binomials**. Polynomials of three terms are called **trinomials**.

Directions: All of the following are polynomial expressions. Place the letter "M" before the monomials. Place the letter "B" before the binomials. Place the letter "T" before the trinomials.

— **21.** 6$y + x$ — **22.** 6y - 2 — **23.** $x + y + a$/b — **24.** 3b - 2a + 6 — **25.** x/b

— **26.** $\frac{2}{3}x$ — **27.** x — **28.** $\frac{1}{3}x + \frac{2}{3}y$ - 8 — **29.** xt + 7/n — **30.** 10xb^2

ADDING POLYNOMIALS

LIKE TERMS

Algebra problems often require adding, subtracting, multiplying, and dividing polynomials.

> **When adding polynomials, *like terms* are added. Like terms have the same variable and the same exponent.**

For example, in the list of terms: $2x^2$, x^2, $10x^2$, $-3x^3$, the first three terms are like terms because they have the same variable and the same exponent. These three may be added together, but $-3x^3$ cannot because the exponent is different, and therefore it is not a like term.

Example 1:

In the polynomial $x^3 + x^2 + 3x^3 + x^2$, the like terms can be added. Adding the like terms $x^3 + 3x^3 = 4x^3$ and $x^2 + x^2 = 2x^2$.

So the like terms are added, and $x^3 + x^2 + 3x^3 + x^2$ becomes $4x^3 + 2x^2$, a simplified form of the original polynomial.

Example 2:

Add $-x^4 + 3y^2 - x^2$ and $3x^4 - 4x^2 + 2y^2$.

One way to add polynomials is to select one of the variables and arrange the like terms in descending power. In this example, the variable x is selected as the variable to use in arranging the like terms in descending power.

So: $-x^4 + 3y^2 - x^2$ becomes $-x^4 - x^2 + 3y^2$ plus $3x^4 - 4x^2 + 2y^2$, which becomes $3x^4 - 4x^2 + 2y^2$.

Adding like terms $-x^4 + 3y^2 - x^2$ plus $3x^4 - 4x^2 + 2y^2$

Simplified $= 2x^4 - 5x^2 + 5y^2$

Example 3:

Add $(-2x^2 + 2x - y^2) - (x^2 + x - y)$.

When adding these polynomials, the parentheses must be removed. Refer to Learning About Parentheses and Brackets on pages 27 and 28 for a further discussion of working with parentheses and brackets. $(-2x^2 + 2x - y^2)$ is assumed to have a positive (+) sign in front of the parentheses, so the parentheses can be removed without changing the signs inside the parentheses.

In the case of $-(x^2 + x - y)$ the parentheses are preceded by a negative (-) sign. In this case, each sign inside the parentheses must be changed when the parentheses are removed. $-(x^2 + x - y)$ is rewritten without the parentheses as $-x^2 - x + y$.

Now the polynomial reads: $-2x^2 + 2x - y^2 - x^2 - x + y$, and you can add like terms. The complete problem is shown below.

$(-2x^2 + 2x - y^2) - (x^2 + x - y) = -2x^2 + 2x - y^2 - x^2 - x + y = -3x^2 + x - y^2 + y$ (simplified).

Name: _____ Date: _____

ADDING POLYNOMIALS (CONTINUED)

Directions: Circle the terms in each group that can be added.

1. $2x^2$ x^3 x^2 y^3 $3x$ 2. $7x^3$ n^5 t^3 x^3 $7x$

3. y^4 $3y^4$ $2xy$ y x^5 4. p^2 p^4 $6x^2$ t^2 $2p^4$

5. t^4 rt^2 $3t^4$ y^3 $10t^4$ 6. s^3 $12s^2$ $4x$ $2x$ s

7. $8y^3$ $5y^3$ y^3 x^3 $2x^3$ 8. k $3k$ t^3 $6k$ $5t^2$

9. y^2 x^2 $2x$ $3y$ t^3 10. x^4 $10x^2$ $8x^5$ $2x^2$ x^2

Directions: Simplify the following by adding like terms.

11. $2x + 3x - 4x =$ _____

12. $10y - 4y =$ _____

13. $(5x) - (2x) =$ _____

14. $(5x) - (-2x) =$ _____

15. $3x^2 - 2x + y^2 + x^2 - x + y^2 =$ _____

16. $-5y^2 + 3x^2 + 2y^2 - x^2 =$ _____

17. $-(-5y^2 + 3x^2) + (-2y^2 - x^2) =$ _____

18. $3x^4 - 2x^3 + x^2 - y^2 + y - 2y^2 + x^3 + y - x^4 + 3y^2 =$ _____

_____

19. $-(-3x^4 + 2x^3 - x^2 + y^2 - y) - (2y^2 - x^3 - y + x^4 - 3y^2) =$ _____

_____

20. $-(-x^2 + y^2 - 3y^3 + x^4) + (-x^3 + y^2 - 2y^3 - 4x^4) =$ _____

_____

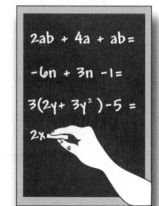

Name: _____ Date: _____

 SUBTRACTING POLYNOMIALS

> **When subtracting polynomials, they are arranged in column form and like terms are subtracted.**

Remember to arrange the polynomials so that like terms will appear in each column.

Example 1: Subtract $3x - 2y$ from $5x + y$
     Step 1: Arrange the polynomials in column form with like terms in the same column.

$$\begin{array}{r} 5x + y \\ -\ \underline{3x - 2y} \end{array} \text{ subtrahend}$$

     Step 2: Change the sign of the terms in the subtrahend. Now add the columns.

$$\begin{array}{r} 5x + y \\ +\ \underline{-3x + 2y} \\ 2x + 3y \end{array} \text{ subtrahend}$$

Example 2: Subtract $(3x^2 - y^2 + z) - (x^2 - y^2 - 2z)$
     Step1: Remove the parentheses. Remember to change the sign inside the parentheses when the parentheses are preceded by a negative (-) sign.
$$(3x^2 - y^2 + z) - (x^2 - y^2 - 2z) = 3x^2 - y^2 + z - x^2 + y^2 + 2z$$
     Step 2: Arrange the like terms in column form and add.

$$\begin{array}{r} 3x^2 - y^2 + z \\ -\ \underline{+x^2 - y^2 - 2z} \end{array} \qquad \begin{array}{r} 3x^2 - y^2 + z \\ +\ \underline{-x^2 + y^2 + 2z} \\ 2x^2 \qquad + 3z \end{array}$$

Directions: Subtract the following polynomials. Arrange in column form. Remember to change the sign of the subtrahend and add.

1. $(2xy - 3x + 4y) - (xy + x - 27) =$

2. $-(4x - 3b) - (x + 2b) =$

3. $(3x^3 - 2x^2 - x + y) - (2x^3 + x^2 + x - y) =$

4. $(5x + 4y - 2a) - (4x + a) =$

5. $(12x^3 + 10y^2 + y) - (x - y^2 - y) =$

6. $(12x^3 + 10y^2 + y) - (x^3 - y^2 - y) =$

7. $-(12x^3 + 10y^2 + y) - (x^3 - y^2 - y) =$

8. $-(12x^3 + 10y^2 + y) + (x^3 - y^2 - y) =$

Name: _____ Date: _____

 MULTIPLYING POLYNOMIALS

When multiplying a polynomial by a *monomial,* each term of the polynomial is multiplied by the monomial. For example, $2(x + y) = 2x + 2y$. When the monomial 2 is multiplied by each term of the polynomial $(x + y)$, the result is $2x + 2y$.

In reviewing exponents, note that: $x^1 = x$; $x^2 = x \cdot x$; $x^3 = x \cdot x \cdot x$; $x^4 = x \cdot x \cdot x \cdot x$; etc.

In learning to multiply polynomials, it is important to review the multiplication of exponents.

Example 1:
Multiply: $x^1 \cdot x^1 = x^{1+1} = x^2$ $y^2 \cdot y^3 = y^{2+3} = y^5$
Multiply: $2x^1 \cdot 3x^1 = 6x^{1+1} = 6x^2$ $3y^2 \cdot 4y^3 = 12y^{2+3} = 12y^5$

Example 2:
Multiply $(x + y)$ times $2 = 2(x + y) = 2x + 2y$
Multiply $(x^2 + y^2)$ times $2x = 2x(x^2 + y^2) = 2x^{1+2} + 2xy^2 = 2x^3 + 2xy^2$

Note: In multiplying the polynomials, the numbers preceding the variables are multiplied as usual. To multiply like variables, add the exponents.

Directions: Multiply the following.

1. $3(x - y) =$ _____ - _____

2. $3x(x + y) =$ _____ + _____

3. $t^2(t^3 - y^2) =$ _____ - _____

4. $-2x(x^2 + x - y) =$ _____

5. $-3y^2(-3xy) =$ _____

6. $5x(-3x^3 + 2x^2 - xy + y) =$ _____

7. $-5x(-3x^3 + 2x^2 - xy + y) =$ _____

8. $-3xy(14xy^2) =$ _____

9. $-3x^2y(-14xy^2) =$ _____

10. $3a^2(2a^3 - 3a^3) =$ _____

Name: _____ Date: _____

MULTIPLYING POLYNOMIALS (CONTINUED)

In all of the problems on the previous page, a monomial was multiplied by a polynomial. However, many times a polynomial is multiplied by a polynomial.

Example 3:

When multiplying a polynomial by a polynomial, arrange the polynomials in column form. Find the product of $(2x - y)(x + y)$. Note the steps in multiplying polynomials.

Multiplying from left to right

Step 1: Multiply x times $2x$
Step 2: Multiply x times $-y$
Step 3: Multiply y times $2x$
Step 4: Multiply y times $-y$

Steps 1 & 2
$2x - y$
$\cdot \quad x$
$\overline{2x^2 - xy}$

Steps 3 & 4
$2x - y$
$\cdot \quad y$
$\overline{2xy - y^2}$

Step 5: Add the partial products: $2x^2 - xy + 2xy - y^2 = 2x^2 + xy - y^2$

Directions: Multiply the following and simplify by adding the partial products.

11. $(3x - 2y)(x + y)$
$3x - 2y \qquad 3x - 2y$
$\cdot \quad x \qquad\quad \cdot \quad y$

12. $(x^2 + 1)(x - y)$

13. $(-3x^2 + y^3)(x^2 - y^2)$

14. $(x - y)(-x - y)$

15. $(-x - y^3)(-x + y)$

16. $(t - x^4)(2t - x^4)$

Name: _____ Date: _____

DIVIDING POLYNOMIALS

When dividing polynomials, the division of like variables becomes very important.

Example 1: To divide like variables x^4/x^2, the exponents are subtracted.
Step 1: Subtract the exponents: $4 - 2 = 2$
Step 2: Rewrite the variable with the exponent 2
$$x^4/x^2 = x^{4-2} = x^2$$

Example 2: Divide x^2/x^4
Step 1: Subtract the exponents: $2 - 4 = -2$
Step 2: Rewrite the variable with the exponent -2
$$x^2/x^4 = x^{2-4} = x^{-2}$$
Step 3: Rewrite x^{-2} as the denominator of a fraction with a numerator 1.
$$1/x^2$$

Example 3: Divide $9x^3y/3xy$
Step 1: Rewrite as $\dfrac{9x^3y}{3xy}$
Step 2: Divide 9 by 3 $= \dfrac{3x^3y}{xy}$
Step 3: Subtract the exponents of like variables
$$x^{3-1} = x^2 \text{ and } y^{1-1} = y^0 = 1$$
Step 4: Rewrite the problem
$\qquad 3x^2$ ($y^0 = 1$: When the variable is 1, it is not rewritten.)

Example 4: Divide $9xy/3x^3y$
Step 1: Rewrite as $\dfrac{9xy}{3x^3y}$
Step 2: Divide 9 by 3 $= \dfrac{3xy}{x^3y}$
Step 3: Subtract the exponents of like variables
$$x^{1-3} = x^{-2} = 1/x^2 \text{ and } y^{1-1} = y^0 = 1$$
Step 4: Rewrite the problem
$\qquad 3 \cdot 1/x^2$ or $\dfrac{3}{x^2}$ ($y^0 = 1$: When the variable is 1, it is not rewritten.)

Directions: Solve the following

1. $x^5/x^3 =$ _____

2. $y^8/y^4 =$ _____

3. $t^2/t =$ _____

4. $4x^3/2x =$ _____

5. $12y^4/3y^3 =$ _____

6. $x^3/x =$ _____

7. $x^3/x^5 =$ _____

8. $y^4/y^8 =$ _____

9. $t/t^2 =$ _____

10. $-4x^3/2x =$ _____

11. $12y^4/-3y^3 =$ _____

12. $-x^3/-x =$ _____

Name: _____   Date: _____

DIVIDING POLYNOMIALS (CONTINUED)

> **When dividing a polynomial by a monomial, divide each term of the polynomial by the monomial.**

Example 5: Divide $(rt + st)/t = \dfrac{rt + st}{t} = \dfrac{1(r\cancel{t})}{\cancel{t}} + \dfrac{1(s\cancel{t})}{\cancel{t}} = r + s$

The polynomial is $rt + st$. Each term rt and st must be divided by the monomial t.

Example 6: Divide $(6x^2y + 4x^3)/2xy = \dfrac{6x^2y}{2xy} + \dfrac{4x^3}{2xy} = \dfrac{\overset{3x^1y^0}{\cancel{6x^2y}}}{\cancel{2xy}} + \dfrac{\overset{2x^2}{\cancel{4x^3}}}{\cancel{2xy}} = \dfrac{3x + 2x^2}{y}$

Directions: Divide the following and simplify.

13. $(14x^4 + 6x^3)/2x =$ **a)** $\dfrac{14x^4}{2x} + \dfrac{6x^3}{2x} =$ **b)** _____ + _____

14. $(3y^2 - 3y)/3y =$ **a)** _____ - _____ =   **b)** _____ - _____

15. $(9r^5 - 12r^3 + 6r)/3r^2 =$ **a)** _____ - _____ + _____ =   **b)** _____ - _____ + _____

16. $(14x^4 + 6x^3)/-2x =$ **a)** _____ + _____ =   **b)** _____ + _____

17. $(3y^2 - 3x)/-3y =$ **a)** _____ - _____ =   **b)** _____ - _____

18. $(-14x^4 + 6x^3)/2x =$ **a)** _____ + _____ =   **b)** _____ + _____

19. $(ab + as)/a =$ **a)** _____ + _____ =   **b)** _____ + _____

20. $(10c - 5a)/5 =$ **a)** _____ - _____ =   **b)** _____ - _____

Name: _____ Date: _____

Quiz IV: Understanding Polynomials

Directions: Match the definition in Column B with its corresponding term in Column A by placing the letter next to the term.

Column A	Column B
_____ **1.** Monomial	**A.** An algebraic expression of one or more terms
_____ **2.** Term	**B.** A polynomial with two terms
_____ **3.** Polynomial	**C.** A polynomial with three terms
_____ **4.** Binomial	**D.** A polynomial with one term
_____ **5.** Trinomial	**E.** An expression referring to a number, variable, or number and variable representing one number

Directions: Circle the like terms in the following list

6. $3x^3$ x^2 $5x^2$ y $3y^3$

Directions: Simplify the following (add or combine).

7. $5y + 10y + 2y^2 - y^2 =$ _____

8. $-(2x^2 - 3x + 5y) + (10x^2 + 4x - 6y) =$ _____

Directions: Simplify the following. To solve, arrange in column form in space to right of problem.

9. $(10x^3 - 3y^3 - 2y^2 + 2) - (-7x^3 - 6y^3 + 4y^2 - 3) =$

Simplified =

10. $(2x^2 + y)(3x^3 - 2y) =$

Simplified =

11. $(8y^4 - 4y^3 - 2y^2)/2y =$

Simplified =

Name: _____ Date: _____

Learning About Equations
WRITTEN AND MATHEMATICAL EXPRESSIONS

An **equation** is a mathematical statement of equality in which two numbers or algebraic expressions are said to be equal. Equations are the primary method of solving problems in algebra. Understanding equations is not difficult. Every day we use mathematical expressions and easily understand them. Some of the English expressions we use and their mathematical counterparts are listed below.

English Expression	Mathematical Expression
Five more than a number	$y + 5$
Five added to a number	$y + 5$
A number is increased by five	$y + 5$
Five less than a number	$y - 5$
Five subtracted from a number	$y - 5$
A number is decreased by five	$y - 5$
Five more than two times a number	$2y + 5$
Five added to two times a number	$2y + 5$
Five less than two times a number	$2y - 5$
Five subtracted from two times a number	$2y - 5$
Five times a number	$5y$
One-fifth of a number	$y \div 5$ or $y/5$

Directions: Read the following written expressions and rewrite them as mathematical expressions. Use the letter y to represent the unknown number.

1. Seven more than a specific number _____

2. Three less than a specific number _____

3. Eight times a specific number _____

4. Three more than five times a specific number _____

5. Five more than one-eighth of a specific number _____

Directions: Change the following sentences into mathematical equations.

6. A number multiplied by five, plus six is equal to 50. _____

7. A number divided by five, less seven is equal to 37. _____

8. If you multiply a number by 13, you get 117. _____

9. Alonzo bought 5 boxes of trading cards. There were the same number in each box. He bought a total of 55 trading cards. _____

10. Mary scored a certain number of points. Emily scored one less than twice as many. Emily scored thirty points. How many points did Mary score? _____

Name: _____ Date: _____

EQUATIONS

You have learned that polynomials like $3 + x$, $x + y$, or $6y$ are called algebraic expressions. In **algebraic expressions**, any numbers can be substituted for the variables used.

An **equation** is a mathematical statement of equality. It states that two numbers or algebraic expressions are equal. The algebraic expressions $3 + x$, $x + y$, and $6y$ are written below as parts of equations.

$$3 + x = 7 \quad x + y = 20 \quad 6y = 42$$

In each case, the algebraic expressions have been connected to another expression by an equal sign. Connect the expressions with an equal ($=$) sign, and you have a mathematical statement of equality or an equation.

In solving equations, it is important to emphasize the equal sign. In solving the equation, you must find numbers that can be substituted for the variable(s) so that the two expressions are equal. **The solutions for the equation must be true.** This means that the solutions found must make the two expressions in the equation equal.

For example, in the equation $3 + x = 7$ if the number 4 is substituted for x, the two expressions are equal. The equation has been solved with a true solution. If you substitute any other whole number for the x, the two expressions are no longer equal.

Directions: Complete the following exercise. Solve the equations below so that there are true solutions to the equations.

1. $5 + y = 9$ Solution: $y =$ _____

2. $5 - x = 4$ Solution: $x =$ _____

3. $s + t = 9$ Solutions: If $s = 4$, then $t =$ _____   If $s = 1$, then $t =$ _____

4. $s - t = 6$ Solutions: If $s = 16$, then $t =$ _____   If $s = 9$, then $t =$ _____

5. $6y = 36$ Solution: $y =$ _____

6. $2x + 5 = 17$ Solution: $x =$ _____

7. $2x + r = 15$ Solutions: If $x = -3$, then $r =$ _____   If $s = 6$, then $r =$ _____

8. $2y - 2 = 12$ Solution: $y =$ _____

9. $2y - x = 12$ Solutions: If $y = 8$, then $x =$ _____   If $y = 10$, then $x =$ _____

10. $15/x = 3$ Solution: $x =$ _____

UNDERSTANDING EQUATIONS

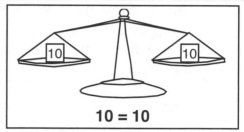

An easy way to understand equations is by visualizing a scale. If both sides of a scale have the same amount of weight, then the scale balances, as in the illustration. An equation can be compared to a scale because both sides of an equation are equal.

10 = 10

Both sides have ten pounds of weight, so the scale is perfectly balanced. It really doesn't matter if the weights on both sides of the scale are each ten-pound blocks or a combination of weights that total ten pounds. If the weight on each side of the scale is equal to the other, then the scale balances as it does in the following illustrations.

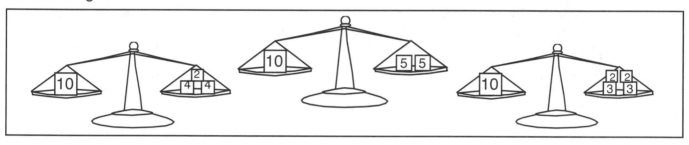

Similarly, an equation is true if it is equal on both sides of the equal sign.

10 = 4 + 4 + 2   **10 = 5 + 5**   **10 = 3 + 3 + 2 + 2**

> **If you do the same thing to both sides of a scale they remain balanced. If you do the same thing to both sides of an equation, they also remain equal.**

Here are some examples of balanced equations.

Example: If you **add** the same number to both sides of an equation, the equation remains true.

$$10 = 10$$
$$10 + 4 = 10 + 4$$
$$14 = 14$$

Example: If you **subtract** the same number from both sides of an equation, the equation remains true.

$$10 = 10$$
$$10 - 4 = 10 - 4$$
$$6 = 6$$

Example: If you **multiply** both sides of an equation by the same number, the equation remains true.

$$10 = 10$$
$$10 \cdot 3 = 10 \cdot 3$$
$$30 = 30$$

Example: If you **divide** both sides of an equation by the same number, the equation remains true.

$$10 = 10$$
$$10 \div 2 = 10 \div 2$$
$$5 = 5$$

Name: _____ Date: _____

 REVIEW OF EQUATION RULES

Here is a review of some of the rules to use when studying equations.

The same number may be added to both sides of an equation, and the equation will remain true.

Example:

Begin with the equation $y - 8 = 23$
Add +8 to each side, and the equation becomes $y - 8 + 8 = 23 + 8$
Which means $y = 31$

Transposition **is the practice of moving a quantity from one side of the equation to the other and changing its sign to the opposite sign.**

Transposition is basically what occurred in the above example. Transposition is often used to change the equation so that the unknown quantity is on one side of the equation and the known quantity on the other. Transposition is also used in the following examples.

Directions: Solve the following. The first one has been completed.

1. $x - 7 = 14$ a) $x - 7 + 7 = 14 + 7$ b) $x = 21$ c) $21 - 7 = 14$

2. $x - 9 = 3$ a) _____   b) _____   c) _____

3. $x - 15 = 55$ a) _____   b) _____   c) _____

4. $x - 18 = 10$ a) _____   b) _____   c) _____

The same number may be subtracted from both sides of an equation, and the equation will remain true.

Example:

Begin with the equation $y + 8 = 23$
Subtract 8 from each side and the equation becomes $y + 8 - 8 = 23 - 8$
Which means $y = 15$

Directions: Solve the following. The first one has been completed.

5. $x + 7 = 14$ a) $x + 7 - 7 = 14 - 7$ b) $x = 7$ c) $7 + 7 = 14$

6. $x + 9 = 23$ a) _____   b) _____   c) _____

7. $x + 15 = 55$ a) _____   b) _____   c) _____

8. $x + 18 = 28$ a) _____   b) _____   c) _____

Name: _____ Date: _____

REVIEW OF EQUATION RULES (CONTINUED)

Each side of an equation may be multiplied by the same number, and the equation will remain true. Zero cannot be used.

Example:

Begin with the equation $\frac{y}{6} = 72$

Multiply each side by 6 and the equation becomes $\frac{y}{6} \cdot 6 = 72 \cdot 6$

Which means $y = 432$

Directions: Solve the following. The first one has been completed for you.

9. $\frac{x}{8} = 2$ a) $\frac{x}{8} \cdot 8 = 2 \cdot 8$ b) $x = 16$ c) Check: $\frac{16}{8} = 2$

10. $\frac{y}{9} = 3$ a) _____   b) _____   c) _____

11. $\frac{y}{2} = 32$ a) _____   b) _____   c) _____

12. $\frac{x}{25} = 125$ a) _____   b) _____   c) _____

13. $\frac{y}{4} = 15$ a) _____   b) _____   c) _____

Both sides of an equation may be divided by the same number, and the equation will remain true. Zero cannot be used.

Example:

Begin with the equation $6y = 72$

Divide each side by 6 and the equation becomes $\frac{6y}{6} = \frac{72}{6}$

Which means $y = 12$

Directions: Solve the following. The first one has been completed.

14. $5x = 25$ a) $\dfrac{5x}{5} = \dfrac{25}{5}$ b) $\dfrac{\cancel{5}x}{\cancel{5}} = \dfrac{\overset{5}{\cancel{25}}}{\cancel{5}}$ c) $x = 5$ d) Check: $5 \cdot 5 = 25$

15. $9y = 576$ a)   b)   c) _____   d) _____

16. $12x = 12$ a)   b)   c) _____   d) _____

17. $10x = 1,000$ a)   b)   c) _____   d) _____

18. $7y = 98$ a)   b)   c) _____   d) _____

Name: _____ Date: _____

LEARNING ABOUT PARENTHESES AND BRACKETS

Many equations will have parentheses and/or brackets that must be removed before solving the equation. When removing parentheses and brackets, it is very important to remember that when the parentheses are preceded by a positive sign (+), the signs inside the parentheses **are not** changed.

Example:

Begin with the equation: $2 + (5x - 1) = 11$
Remove parentheses and multiply each term inside by 1. $2 + 5x \cdot 1 - 1 \cdot 1 = 11$
The equation becomes: $2 + 5x - 1 = 11$
Subtract -2 and +1 from each side of the equation. $+2 - 2 + 5x - 1 + 1 = 11 - 2 + 1$
The equation becomes: $5x = 10$
Divide each side of the equation by 5. $5x \div 5 = 10 \div 5$
Which means $x = 2$

Example:

Begin with the equation $3 + (2x + 1) = 16$
Becomes $3 + 2x + 1 = 16$
Becomes $-3 + 3 + 2x + 1 - 1 = 16 - 3 - 1$
Becomes $\dfrac{2x}{2} = \dfrac{12}{2}$
Becomes $x = 6$
Check $3 + 2 \cdot 6 + 1 = 16$ $(16 = 16)$

Directions: Solve the following. The first one has been completed.

1. $5 + 2(x + 2) = 21$

  a) $5 + 2x + 4 = 21$

  b) $-5 + 5 + 2x + 4 - 4 = 21 - 5 - 4$

  c) $\dfrac{2x}{2} = \dfrac{12}{2}$

  d) $x = 6$

  e) check: $5 + 2 \cdot 6 + 4 = 21$ $(21 = 21)$

2. $1 + (3x - 3) = 1$

  a)

  b)

  c)

  d) _____

  e) check: _____

3. $8 + 3(y + 2) = 20$

  a)

  b)

  c)

  d) _____

  e) check: _____

4. $-3 + 2(y - 3) = -3$

  a)

  b)

  c)

  d) _____

  e) check: _____

Name: _____ Date: _____

LEARNING ABOUT PARENTHESES AND BRACKETS (CONTINUED)

It is also important to remember that when the parentheses are preceded by a negative sign (-), the signs inside the parentheses **are** changed.

Example:

Begin with the equation: $2 - (5x - 1) = -7$
Remove parentheses and multiply each term inside by -1.
$$2 + 5x \cdot (-1) - 1 \cdot (-1) = -7$$
The equation becomes: $2 - 5x + 1 = -7$
Subtract 2 and 1 from each side of the equation. $-2 + 2 - 5x + 1 - 1 = -7 - 2 - 1$
The equation becomes: $-5x = -10$
Divide each side of the equation by -5. $\dfrac{-5x}{-5} = \dfrac{-10}{-5}$

Which means: $x = 2$

Example:

Begin with the equation: $3 - (2x + 1) = -16$
Becomes: $3 - 2x - 1 = -16$
Becomes: $-3 + 3 - 2x - 1 + 1 = -16 - 3 + 1$
Becomes: $-2x = -18$
Becomes: $\dfrac{-2x}{-2} = \dfrac{-18}{-2}$
Becomes: $x = 9$
Check: $3 - (2 \cdot 9 + 1) = -16$

Directions: Solve the following. The first one has been completed.

5. $5 - 2(x + 2) = -9$
    a) $5 - 2x - 4 = -9$
    b) $-5 + 5 - 2x - 4 + 4 = -9 - 5 + 4$
    c) $\dfrac{-2x}{-2} = \dfrac{-10}{-2}$
    d) $x = 5$
    e) check: $5 - 2 \cdot 5 - 4 = -9$

6. $3 - 6(x + 3) = 33$
    a)
    b)
    c)
    d) _____
    e) check: _____

7. $-4(2x - 2) = -16$
    a)
    b)
    c)
    d) _____
    e) check: _____

8. $3x - (2x + 4) = -2$
    a)
    b)
    c)
    d) _____
    e) check: _____

Name: _____ Date: _____

ORDER OF OPERATIONS

When solving equations, the order in which you perform the operations is very important. The operations are addition, subtraction, multiplication, and division. When equations have mathematical expressions with parentheses, it is important to remove the parentheses before performing the operations. You have learned that when the parentheses are preceded by a positive sign, the signs inside the parentheses are not changed when the parentheses are removed. When the parentheses are preceded by a negative sign, the signs inside the parentheses are changed when the parentheses are removed.

Example 1:

In an equation or mathematical expression, begin with the equation:

$$3 - (7 + 3) + \left(\tfrac{2}{2}\right) = x$$

1. Work from left to right $3 - (7 + 3) + \left(\tfrac{2}{2}\right) = x$

2. Left to right, remove parentheses/attach correct signs $3 - 7 - 3 + \tfrac{2}{2} = x$
3. From left to right, complete any multiplication and division $3 - 7 - 3 + 1 = x$
4. From left to right, complete the addition and subtraction $3 - 7 - 3 + 1 = x$
5. Which means: $-6 = x$
6. Simplify if necessary:

Example 2 :

Begin with the equation: $6a(3 + 1) + \tfrac{28}{7} = x$

1. Left to right, remove parentheses/attach correct signs: $18a + 6a + \tfrac{28}{7} = x$
2. Left to right, complete any multiplication/division: $18a + 6a + 4 = x$
3. Left to right, complete addition/subtraction $24a + 4 = x$
4. Simplify if necessary: $4(6a + 1) = x$

Directions: Simplify the following.

1. $8 - (4 + 3 + 1) + \left(\tfrac{8}{4}\right) = x$ **2.** $10 + (8 + 1) - 2(-5) = x$ **3.** $-1(6) + -2\left(\tfrac{8}{4}\right) = x$

a)   a)   a)

b)   b)   b)

c)   c)   c)

d)   d)   d)

4. $5(x - y) - z = x$ **5.** $9x - 2(3a + a) - 3\left(\tfrac{4}{2}a\right) = x$ **6.** $-4x - (8 \cdot 3) = x$

a)   a)   a)

b)   b)   b)

c)   c)   c)

d)   d)   d)

Name: _____ Date: _____

Quiz V: Learning About Equations

Directions: Fill in the blanks in the following selection with the appropriate word chosen from the list below. Words may be used more than once.

equality	$2x + 1 = 7$	parentheses	zero	positive	left/right
operations	addition	subtraction	multiplication	division	added
subtracted	divided	multiplied	simplified	equal	negative
mathematical statement		algebraic expressions			

An equation is a **1.** _____ _____ of **2.** _____, like

3. __ + __ = __. An equation is made up of two **4.** _____ _____

connected by the **5.** _____ sign, which is the sign of **6.** _____.

The same number may be **7.** _____ to each side of an equation without changing

the equation. The same number may be **8.** _____ from each side of an equation

without changing the equation. Excepting for **9.** _____, each side of the equation may be

multiplied or **10.** _____ by the same number without changing the equation.

In simplifying an equation, one must always work from **11.** _____ to _____.

First the **12.** _____ are removed. When the parentheses are preceded by a

13. _____ sign, the signs inside the parentheses are changed when the parentheses

are removed. When the parentheses are preceded by a **14.** _____ sign, the signs

inside the parentheses are not changed when the parentheses are removed.

Once the parentheses have been removed, the order of operations from **15.** _____

to _____ are first **16.** _____ and _____ and then

17. _____ and _____. Following the operations, the terms are

combined, and the resulting mathematical expression is **18.** _____.

Directions: Simplify the following.

19. $6x - (2 - x) + 3 = x$ _____

20. $2y + (\frac{10}{5}x) - 2(3 + 1) = x$ _____

Directions: Match the the definition in Column B with the corresponding item in Column A.

Column A		Column B
_____	**21.** $6y + 1 = 13$	**A.** Monomial
_____	**22.** $6x$	**B.** Algebraic expression
_____	**23.** $6a + 1$	**C.** Equation
_____	**24.** $6y + 2$	**D.** Cannot be used to divide each side of an equation
_____	**25.** Zero	**E.** Simplified is $2(3y + 1)$

Name: _____ Date: _____

Understanding and Using Exponents

There are times when a number is used as a factor several times. A number may be multiplied by itself once or several times. To multiply a number by itself once is called **squaring** a number. This also may be called raising the number to its **second power.** If the number is multiplied by itself three times, we say the number is raised to its **third power** and so on. The power of a number is the product resulting from multiplying a number by itself a number of times. Raising a number to a specific power is exactly the *opposite* process of finding the root of a number.

$5 \cdot 5 =$	25	Five to the second power, also called five squared
$5 \cdot 5 \cdot 5 =$	125	Five to the third power, also called five cubed
$5 \cdot 5 \cdot 5 \cdot 5 =$	625	Five to the fourth power
$5 \cdot 5 \cdot 5 \cdot 5 \cdot 5 =$	3,125	Five to the fifth power

The number or variable with the exponent is called the **base.** The **exponent** number is smaller and is placed above and to the right of the first. The exponent shows how many times the first number should be used as a factor.

$$\text{Base} \longrightarrow 5^4 \longleftarrow \text{Exponent}$$

Using the above examples, here is how the numbers should be written with exponents.

$5 \cdot 5$	$= 5^2 =$	Five to the second power
$5 \cdot 5 \cdot 5$	$= 5^3 =$	Five to the third power
$5 \cdot 5 \cdot 5 \cdot 5$	$= 5^4 =$	Five to the fourth power
$5 \cdot 5 \cdot 5 \cdot 5 \cdot 5$	$= 5^5 =$	Five to the fifth power

The base and exponent are always read in a particular way.

> *Example:* 2^2 is read as "two to the second power." Note the base is read as the numeral it represents. The exponent is read as "to a power."

> *Example:* 5^3 is read as "five to the third power."

Directions: For each of the following, fill in the blank with the number the base and exponent represent. The first one has been completed.

1. 4^3 = 64

2. $3^3 =$ _____

3. 7^2 = _____

4. $10^5 =$ _____

5. $14^3 =$ _____

6. $8^8 =$ _____

7. $11^7 =$ _____

8. $7^9 =$ _____

Directions: In the blanks beside each base and exponent, write the statement that the term describes.

9. 5^3 is read as: _____

10. 4^4 is read as: _____

11. 7^5 is read as: _____

12. 42^1 is read as: _____

Name: _____ Date: _____

EXPONENTS, BASES, AND FACTORS

When learning about exponents, it is important to know the meaning of the terms **exponent, base,** and **factor.**

• **Exponent:** The small number appearing to the right and above a number or variable.

For example, 4^2, 3^5, 7^3, 10^4, x^9, y^6, $2x^3$, 4^5x^2 are all either a number, a variable, or a number and variable with exponents. The exponent is the small number to the right and above the number or variable.

• **Base:** The number or variable with the exponent is called the base.

For example, the numbers, variables, or numbers and variables in bold are each a base: $\mathbf{4}^2$, $\mathbf{3}^5$, $\mathbf{7}^3$, $\mathbf{10}^4$, $\boldsymbol{x}^9$, $\boldsymbol{y}^6$, $\mathbf{2}\boldsymbol{x}^3$, $\mathbf{4}^5\boldsymbol{x}^2$.

• **Factor:** The numbers that are multiplied together to get a product.

For example, 3 and 2 are factors of 6 because $3 \cdot 2 = 6$. The factors 3 and 4 are factors of 12 because $3 \cdot 4 = 12$. Three is a factor of 9 because $3 \cdot 3 = 9$.

The **exponent** tells you how many times the **base** is to be multiplied as a **factor.**
For example, 2^2 tells you to multiply $2 \cdot 2 = 4$, 2^3 tells you to multiply $2 \cdot 2 \cdot 2 = 8$, 4^4 tells you to multiply $4 \cdot 4 \cdot 4 \cdot 4 = 256$

Sometimes you will find a variable like x or y with an exponent, for example, x^2 or y^2. In this case, the base is the number assigned for x or y.

Directions: Solve the following.

1. $2^2 =$ _____
2. $2^3 =$ _____
3. $2^4 =$ _____
4. $2^6 =$ _____

5. $3^2 =$ _____
6. $3^3 =$ _____
7. $3^4 =$ _____
8. $3^5 =$ _____

9. $4^2 =$ _____
10. $4^3 =$ _____
11. $4^4 =$ _____
12. $4^5 =$ _____

13. $10^2 =$ _____
14. $10^3 =$ _____
15. $10^4 =$ _____
16. $10^5 =$ _____

Directions: In blank a) place the base and exponent the statement describes. In blank b) place the number the base and exponent represent. The first one is completed.

17. Eight to the second power.   a) 8^2 equals   b) 64

18. Twelve to the eighth power.   a) _____   equals   b) _____

19. Two to the sixth power.   a) _____   equals   b) _____

20. Four to the zero power.   a) _____   equals   b) _____

21. Three to the fourth power.   a) _____   equals   b) _____

22. Seven to the first power.   a) _____   equals   b) _____

Name: _____ Date: _____

EXPONENTS IN ALGEBRAIC EXPRESSIONS

Algebraic expressions are often written with variables and exponents. When a variable appears with an exponent, the variable must be assigned a numerical value before the problem can be solved.

Example: To solve x^2, a numerical value must be assigned to the variable x.
Let x equal 5. Then $x^2 = 5^2 = 25$. If x equals 3, then $x^2 = 3^2 = 9$

Directions: Solve the following.

1. $x = 2$ then $x^2 =$ _____   **2.** $x = 3$ then $x^3 =$ _____   **3.** $x = 5$ then $x^5 =$ _____

4. $y = 3$ then $y^3 + 1 =$ ___   **5.** $y = 4$ then $y^4 - 1 =$ ___   **6.** $x = 2; y = 2$ then $x^2 + y^2 =$ ___

7. $x = 3$ then $x^2 + x =$ ___   **8.** $y = 4$ then $y^3 - y =$ ___   **9.** $t = 4$ then $t^2 =$ _____

Directions: The following algebraic expressions include constants, variables, and exponents. To solve the following, let $x = 4; y = 3$.

10. $3x^2 =$ _____   **11.** $2x^3 + 2 =$ _____   **12.** $3x^2 + 2y =$ _____

Solve the following: $x = 5; y = 3$

13. $\dfrac{2x^2}{2} + 3y^2 =$ _____   **14.** $4x^3 - \dfrac{y^3}{9} + 2 =$ _____   **15.** $\dfrac{1 + y^2}{x^2} =$ _____

LOOKING FOR PATTERNS WHEN USING EXPONENTS

Directions: Write the answer to each of the following on the blank next to the problem. The first one has been completed.

16. $3^1 = 3$ **17.** $3^2 =$ _____   **18.** $3^3 =$ _____   **19.** $3^4 =$ _____

20. The answer in Problem 18 is   a) 1   b) 2   c) 3   d) 4   times greater than the answer in Problem 17.

When working with exponents, it is important to remember that any base with an exponent of 0 is equal to 1. $3^0 = 1$ $x^0 = 1$

Directions: Solve the following.

21. a) $2^0 =$ ___ b) $3^0 =$ ___ c) $4^0 =$ ___   **22.** a) $2^3 =$ ___ b) $2^2 =$ ___ c) $2^1 =$ ___ d) $2^0 =$ ___

23. When the exponent for the base numeral 2 in Problem 22 is *decreased* by 1, the answer is
a) $\frac{1}{3}$ b) $\frac{1}{2}$ c) $\frac{1}{4}$ d) $\frac{1}{5}$ the original exponent.

Name: _____ Date: _____

DEALING WITH NEGATIVE EXPONENTS AND NEGATIVE BASES

All of the base numbers previously have had positive exponents. However, many base numbers will have negative exponents. In the example below, all of the base two numerals in bold have a negative exponent.

$$2^5 \quad 2^4 \quad 2^3 \quad 2^2 \quad 2^1 \quad 2^0 \quad \mathbf{2^{-1}} \quad \mathbf{2^{-2}} \quad \mathbf{2^{-3}} \quad \mathbf{2^{-4}} \quad \mathbf{2^{-5}}$$

> You have learned how to handle base numbers with a positive exponent. The rule for using negative exponents is: **Rewrite the base and exponent as a fraction with a numerator of one. Note that the exponent and base will both be positive.**

Example: 2^{-2} is rewritten as $\frac{1}{2^2}$ or $\frac{1}{4}$; 4^{-3} is rewritten as $\frac{1}{4^3}$ or $\frac{1}{64}$

Directions: Rewrite the following. In blank a) write the base and negative exponent as a fraction with a numerator of one. In blank b) rewrite the fraction without the exponent. The first one has been completed.

1. $2^{-2} = \frac{1}{2^2} = \frac{1}{4}$ **2.** $3^{-4} = $ _____ $= $ _____   **3.** $4^{-3} = $ _____ $= $ _____

4. $6^{-3} = $ _____ $= $ _____   **5.** $5^{-3} = $ _____ $= $ _____   **6.** $10^{-2} = $ _____ $= $ _____

Sometimes exponents will be found with a negative base numeral. It will be important to use the following rules.

> When a *positive base* number is raised to an even or odd power, the base number will always remain positive.

Example: $2^2 = 4$; $2^3 = 8$; $2^4 = 16$; $2^5 = 32$; $2^6 = 64$

> When a *negative base* number is raised to an even power, the base number will become positive.

Example: $-2^2 = 4$; $-2^4 = 16$; $-2^6 = 64$; $-2^8 = 256$; $-2^{10} = 1,024$

> When a *negative base* number is raised to an odd power, the base number will remain negative.

Example: $-2^3 = -8$; $-2^5 = -32$; $-2^7 = -128$; $-2^9 = -512$

Directions: Solve the following.

7. $-3^2 = $ _____   **8.** $-3^5 = $ _____   **9.** $3^3 = $ _____   **10.** $-4^3 = $ _____   **11.** $5^3 = $ _____

12. $-2^9 = $ _____   **13.** $-8^3 = $ _____   **14.** $-5^2 = $ _____   **15.** $-2^4 = $ _____

Name: _____ Date: _____

ADDING, SUBTRACTING, AND MULTIPLYING EXPONENTS

Variables and numbers with exponents will occur frequently in algebraic expressions.

When the *base numbers* or *variables* are the same, the exponents can be added.

In problems where you are multiplying numbers or variables with the same base, the exponents can be added. To multiply powers of the same base, add their exponents.

Examples: 3^2 times $3^1 = 3^2 \cdot 3^1 = 3^{2+1} = 3^3; 3 \cdot 3 \cdot 3 = 27$

x^2 times $x^2 = x^2 \cdot x^2 = x^{2+2} = x^4$

$5^3 \cdot 5^2 = 5^5$
$5^3 = 125; 5^2 = 25$
$5^3 \cdot 5^2 = 5^{3+2} = 5^5 = 3,125$
$125 \cdot 25 = 3,125$

Note in all of the examples the **bases** or **variables** to be multiplied were the same.

Directions: Solve the following multiplication problems. Add the exponents and raise the base number to the indicated exponent. Place the answers on the blanks a), b), and c). Only a) and b) can be answered for those with variables. The first one is completed.

1. $5^2 \cdot 5^1 =$ exponents added equals **a)** 5^{2+1} rewritten as **b)** 5^3 equals **c)** 125

2. $6^3 \cdot 6^2 =$ exponents added equals **a)** _____   rewritten as **b)** _____   equals **c)** _____

3. $7^3 \cdot 7^5 =$ exponents added equals **a)** _____   rewritten as **b)** _____   equals **c)** _____

4. $x^3 \cdot x^2 =$ exponents added equals **a)** _____   rewritten as **b)** _____

5. $y^1 \cdot y^4 =$ exponents added equals **a)** _____   rewritten as **b)** _____

6. $r^4 \cdot r^2 =$ exponents added equals **a)** _____   rewritten as **b)** _____

Many times exponents will appear in algebraic expressions like the following.
$$(4^2)^2 \text{ or } (a^2)^3$$
One can solve $(4^2)^2$ by first raising the 4 inside the parentheses to the second power and then raising the answer to the second power.
$$(4 \cdot 4)^2 = (16)^2 = 16 \cdot 16 = 256$$
However, there is another way to solve this problem. You can multiply the exponents and then solve the problem.
$$(4^2)^2 = 4^{2 \cdot 2} = 4^4 = 4 \cdot 4 \cdot 4 \cdot 4 = 256$$

Name: _____ Date: _____

ADDING, SUBTRACTING, AND MULTIPLYING EXPONENTS (CONTINUED)

Directions: Raise the base number or variable to the indicated power by multiplying the exponents. The first one has been completed.

7. $(2^2)^3$ = **a)** $2^{2 \cdot 3}$ = **b)** 2^6 = **c)** 64

8. $(2^4)^2$ = **a)** _____ = **b)** _____ = **c)** _____

9. $(10^3)^2$ = **a)** _____ = **b)** _____ = **c)** _____

10. $(7^1)^5$ = **a)** _____ = **b)** _____ = **c)** _____

11. $(5^3)^3$ = **a)** _____ = **b)** _____ = **c)** _____

12. $(12^2)^2$ = **a)** _____ = **b)** _____ = **c)** _____

13. $(3^3)^4$ = **a)** _____ = **b)** _____ = **c)** _____

14. If "a" equals 2, then $(a^5)^2$ = **a)** _____ = **b)** _____ = **c)** _____

15. If "x" equals 3, then $(x^2)^2$ = **a)** _____ = **b)** _____ = **c)** _____

16. If "y" equals 6, then $(y^1)^3$ = **a)** _____ = **b)** _____ = **c)** _____

Numbers or variables with exponents are often found in division problems, as well.

> **When dividing numbers or variables with exponents, the exponent in the dividend is subtracted from the exponent in the divisor.**

Example: $5^3 \div 5^2 = 5^{3-2} = 5^1 = 5$ or $5^2 \div 5^3 = 5^{2-3} = 5^{-1} = \dfrac{1}{5^1} = \dfrac{1}{5}$

$x^5 \div x^2 = x^{5-2} = x^3$ or $x^3 \div x^5 = x^{3-5} = x^{-2} = \dfrac{1}{x^2}$

Directions: Solve the following. The first one has been completed.

17. $6^4 \div 6^2 =$ **a)** 6^{4-2} = **b)** 6^2 = **c)** 36

18. $7^5 \div 7^4 =$ **a)** _____ = **b)** _____ = **c)** _____

19. $2^6 \div 2^3 =$ **a)** _____ = **b)** _____ = **c)** _____

20. $4^2 \div 4^5 =$ **a)** _____ = **b)** _____ = **c)** _____ = **d)** _____

21. $3^1 \div 3^6 =$ **a)** _____ = **b)** _____ = **c)** _____ = **d)** _____

22. $x^4 \div x^2 =$ **a)** _____ = **b)** _____

23. $y^6 \div y^3 =$ **a)** _____ = **b)** _____

24. $x^4 \div x^6 =$ **a)** _____ = **b)** _____ = **c)** _____

25. $y^7 \div y^8 =$ **a)** _____ = **b)** _____ = **c)** _____

Name: _____ Date: _____

Quiz VI: Understanding and Using Exponents

Directions: Complete the exercises as directed below.

Write the statement that describes how the base and exponent would be read aloud.

1. 4^6 = _____

2. 3^5 = _____

3. 2^4 = _____

Write the number of factors in each expression on blank a) and list the factors on blank b).

4. 5^3 a) ____ b) _____   **5.** 10^5 a) ____ b) _____

6. 3^6 a) ____ b) _____   **7.** y^4 a) ____ b) _____

Raise each of the following to the indicated power

8. 5^3 = ____   **9.** 4^0 = ____   **10.** 10^4 = ____   **11.** 2^6 = ____   **12.** 4^3 = ____

Raise each of the variables to the indicated power.

13. If $x = 4$, then x^2 = ____   **14.** If $y = 9$, then y^0 = ____   **15.** If t equals 5, then t^3 = ____

Solve the following.

16. If $x = 2$, then $3x^2$ = _____   **17.** If $y = 3$, then $10y^3$ = _____

18. If t equals 4, then $6t^2$ = _____

Rewrite each of the following as a fraction with a numerator of one. Raise the base to the indicated power.

19. 2^{-2} = ____ = ____   **20.** 3^{-1} = ____ = ____   **21.** 5^{-2} = ____ = ____

Complete the following.

22. 5^4 = ___ 5^3 = ___ 5^2 = ___ 5^1 = ___ 5^0 = ___ 5^{-1} = ___ 5^{-2} = ___ 5^{-3} = ___ 5^{-4} = ___

Refer to Question 22 and answer the following.

23. Increasing the exponent by one increases the numerical value of the base number 5

   a) 2 times   **b)** 5 times   **c)** 3 times   **d)** 4 times.

24. When the exponent for the base numeral 5 is *decreased* by 1, the answer is

   a) $\frac{1}{3}$ **b)** $\frac{1}{2}$ **c)** $\frac{1}{4}$ **d)** $\frac{1}{5}$ the original exponent.

Solve the following.

25. $9^2 \cdot 9^5$ = _____   **26.** $11^4 \cdot 11^1$ = _____

27. $(5^4)^2$ = _____   **28.** $(7^2)^3$ = _____

29. $4^8 \div 4^2$ = _____   **30.** $4^2 \div 4^8$ = _____

Learning About Radicals and Roots

Radicals are often used in algebra in order to solve problems. Before you can solve such problems, it is necessary to find the root of the numbers or variables under the radical.

The $\sqrt{}$ is the **radical sign**. The number or variable under the radical sign is the **radicand**. The **index** is the number that indicates the root that is to be found. The index indicates that you are to find the square root, cube root, fourth root, fifth root, and so on.

Index
$$\sqrt[3]{125} \text{ ——— } \textbf{Radicand}$$
|
Radical

In the study of exponents, a number is *raised* to a given power.

Example: 5 raised to the second power is written as 5^2 or $5 \cdot 5$, which equals 25.

The inverse operation of raising a number to a power is extracting the root of a number.

Example: Find the square root of 25. **The square root is the number that multiplied times itself will produce 25.**

$$\sqrt[2]{25}$$

In the above example the radical is the sign $\sqrt{}$.
The radicand is the number 25.
The index is the number 2, indicating the square root.
Solution: The square root of 25 is 5. $5 \cdot 5 = 25$

The index is a very important number used in the process of finding the root. The index tells the root that is to be found. The index for the square root is the number 2. Often this index is omitted. Therefore, when the square root is to be found, the index 2 will usually not appear in the radical. In all other roots, such as the cube root or the fourth root, the index number must be included in the radical.

Examples:

$\sqrt[2]{4}$ or $\sqrt{4}$ says "find the square root of 4." $= 2$ $\qquad$ $(2^2 = 2 \cdot 2 = 4)$

$\sqrt[3]{8}$ says, "find the cube root of 8." $= 2$ $\qquad$ $(2^3 = 2 \cdot 2 \cdot 2 = 8)$

$\sqrt[4]{16}$ says, "find the fourth root of 16." $= 2$ $\qquad$ $(2^4 = 2 \cdot 2 \cdot 2 \cdot 2 = 16)$

$\sqrt[5]{32}$ says, "find the fifth root of 32." $= 2$ $\qquad$ $(2^5 = 2 \cdot 2 \cdot 2 \cdot 2 \cdot 2 = 32)$

$\sqrt[6]{64}$ says, "find the sixth root of 64." $= 2$ $\qquad$ $(2^6 = 2 \cdot 2 \cdot 2 \cdot 2 \cdot 2 \cdot 2 = 64)$

Name: _____ Date: _____

 NUMBER OF FACTORS

When finding the root of a number, you are finding how many times a number should be used as a factor when that number is the only factor used.

> *Example:* Find the square root of 25. $\sqrt{25} = 5 \cdot 5$ (five used as a factor two times)
>
> Find the cube root of 125. $\sqrt[3]{125} = 5 \cdot 5 \cdot 5$ (five used as a factor three times)
>
> Find the sixth root of 64. $\sqrt[6]{64} = 2 \cdot 2 \cdot 2 \cdot 2 \cdot 2 \cdot 2$ (two used as a factor six times)

Directions: Complete the following. Find the indicated root and write the answer on blank a), and on blank b) indicate the number of times the answer is to be used as a factor. The first one has been completed for you.

1. $\sqrt[4]{81}$ = **a)** 3   **b)** $3 \cdot 3 \cdot 3 \cdot 3$

2. $\sqrt[3]{125}$ = **a)** _____   **b)** _____

3. $\sqrt[4]{256}$ = **a)** _____   **b)** _____

4. $\sqrt[5]{1{,}024}$ = **a)** _____   **b)** _____

5. $\sqrt[2]{9}$ = **a)** _____   **b)** _____

All of the problems you have solved so far resulted in a **rational** number. However, there are times when the root of a problem is found that the answer is an **irrational** number.

> *Rational* numbers are numbers that can be written as the quotient of fractions. Rational numbers can be expressed with finite, non-repeating decimals or with repeating decimals. Examples: a) $\frac{3}{4} = 0.75$ b) $\frac{2}{3} = 0.666666666666...$
>
> *Irrational* numbers are numbers that cannot be written as fractions. When an irrational number is written in decimal form, the decimal is an infinite, non-repeating decimal. An irrational number is a number with an infinite number of digits. *Pi* or 3.14159265... is a non-repeating decimal. It is an irrational number.

Solve the following. Write the answer on blank a), the term rational or irrational on blank b), and the number of times the answer is used as a factor on blank c). The first one has been completed.

6. $\sqrt[2]{2} =$ **a)** 1.414213562...   **b)** irrational   **c)** 2

7. $\sqrt[2]{3} =$ **a)** _____   **b)** _____   **c)** _____

8. $\sqrt[5]{25} =$ **a)** _____   **b)** _____   **c)** _____

9. $\sqrt[3]{8} =$ **a)** _____   **b)** _____   **c)** _____

10. $\sqrt[2]{38} =$ **a)** _____   **b)** _____   **c)** _____

Name: _____ Date: _____

ADDING AND SUBTRACTING RADICALS

It is often easier to solve problems with more than one radical if the radicals in the expression can be combined.

Radicals can be added if the indexes and radicands are the same.

Example 1: $2\sqrt{5} + 4\sqrt{5}$ can be added. The radicands are both the same (5), and both indexes indicate the square root is to be found.

Example 2: $2\sqrt{5} + 4\sqrt[3]{5}$ cannot be added. The radicands are the same, but the first radicand has an index for the square root, and the second radicand has an index for the cube root.

When adding radicals, the **coefficients** are added. In Example 1 above, the coefficients are the numbers **2** and **4.**

Step 1: Add the coefficients: $2 + 4$

Step 2: Rewrite the answer as: $6\sqrt{5}$

$$2\sqrt{5} + 4\sqrt{5} = 2 + 4 = 6\sqrt{5}$$

Radicals can be subtracted if the indexes and radicands are the same. When subtracting radicals, the coefficients are subtracted.

Example: $5\sqrt{7} - 3\sqrt{7}$ can be subtracted. The indexes are the same and the radicands are the same.

Step 1: Subtract the coefficients: $5 - 3 = 2$

Step 2: Rewrite as $2\sqrt{7}$

$$5\sqrt{7} - 3\sqrt{7} = 5 - 3 = 2\sqrt{7}$$

When the radical has a coefficient of 1, the number 1 is not written before the radical. However, when adding or subtracting, it is added or subtracted as 1.

Examples: $3\sqrt{4} + \sqrt{4} = 3 + 1\sqrt{4} = 4\sqrt{4}$ $\qquad$ $3\sqrt{4} - \sqrt{4} = 3 - 1\sqrt{4} = 2\sqrt{4}$

Directions: Solve the following problems.

1. $2\sqrt{5} + \sqrt{5} =$ ___ + ___ $\sqrt{}$ = ___ $\sqrt{}$

2. $5\sqrt{13} + \sqrt{13} =$ ___ + ___ $\sqrt{}$ = ___ $\sqrt{}$

3. $12\sqrt{156} + 3\sqrt{156} =$ ___ + ___ $\sqrt{}$ = ___ $\sqrt{}$

4. $\sqrt{2} + \sqrt{2} + 3\sqrt{2} =$ ___ + ___ + ___ $\sqrt{}$ = ___ $\sqrt{}$

5. $5\sqrt{7} - 4\sqrt{7} =$ ___ - ___ $\sqrt{}$ = ___ $\sqrt{}$

6. $9\sqrt{8} - \sqrt{8} =$ ___ - ___ $\sqrt{}$ = ___ $\sqrt{}$

7. $\sqrt{12} - \sqrt{12} =$ ___ - ___ $\sqrt{}$ = ___ $\sqrt{}$

8. $6\sqrt{10} - 3\sqrt{10} - 2\sqrt{10} =$ ___ - ___ - ___ $\sqrt{}$ = ___ $\sqrt{}$

9. $6\sqrt{10} + 3\sqrt{10} - 2\sqrt{10} =$ ___ + ___ - ___ $\sqrt{}$ = ___ $\sqrt{}$

10. $\sqrt{3} + 3\sqrt{3} - 2\sqrt{3} =$ ___ + ___ - ___ $\sqrt{}$ = ___ $\sqrt{}$

Name: _____   Date: _____

MULTIPLYING AND DIVIDING RADICALS

Radicals can be multiplied as you would multiply whole numbers. When multiplying radicals, the *indexes* must be the same. *However*, the radicands can be different numbers or variables.

Example 1: $\sqrt{5} \cdot \sqrt{5} = 5 \cdot 5 = 25$ so $\sqrt{5} \cdot \sqrt{5} = \sqrt{25} = 5$

Example 2: $\sqrt[3]{9} \cdot \sqrt[3]{3} = 9 \cdot 3 = 27$ so $\sqrt[3]{9} \cdot \sqrt[3]{3} = \sqrt[3]{27} = 3$

It is important to note that the indexes are the same in each example.

Directions: Solve the following. Complete blanks a), b), and c). In blank c) indicate if the answer in blank b) is rational or irrational. If a variable is under the radical, answer only blank a). The first one has been completed.

1. $\sqrt{4} \cdot \sqrt{4} =$ a) $\sqrt{16}$ = b)   4   c)   rational
2. $\sqrt{2} \cdot \sqrt{8} =$ a) $\sqrt{}$ = b) _____   c) _____
3. $3\sqrt{5} \cdot 3\sqrt{25} =$ a) ___ $\sqrt{}$ = b) _____   c) _____
4. $2\sqrt{x} \cdot 2\sqrt{y} \cdot 2\sqrt{z} =$ a) ___ $\sqrt{}$
5. $4\sqrt{4} \cdot 4\sqrt{6} \cdot 4\sqrt{2} =$ a) ___ $\sqrt{}$ = b) _____   c) _____
6. $\sqrt[3]{2} \cdot \sqrt[3]{4} \cdot 8\sqrt[3]{2} =$ a) ___ $\sqrt{}$ = b) _____   c) _____

Radicals can be divided as you would divide whole numbers. When dividing radicals, the *indexes* must be the same. However, the radicands can be different numbers or variables.

Example 1: $\sqrt{32} \div \sqrt{2} = \frac{32}{2} = \sqrt{16} = 4 =$ rational number

Example 2: $\sqrt{4} \div \sqrt{2} = \frac{4}{2} = \sqrt{2} = 1.414213562 =$ irrational number

Example 3: $\sqrt[3]{81} \div \sqrt[3]{3} = \frac{81}{3} = \sqrt[3]{27} = 3 =$ rational number

It is important to note that the indexes are the same in each example.

Directions: Solve the following. Complete blanks a), b), c), and d). Indicate in blank d) whether the answer in blank c) is rational or irrational. If variables are present, you can only complete blanks a) and b). The first one has been completed.

7. $\sqrt{18} \div \sqrt{2} =$ a) $\frac{18}{2}$ = b) $\sqrt{9}$ = c) 3   d)   rational
8. $\sqrt{48} \div \sqrt{2} =$ a) _____   = b) $\sqrt{}$ = c) _____   d) _____
9. $\sqrt{16} \div \sqrt{4} =$ a) _____   = b) $\sqrt{}$ = c) _____   d) _____
10. $\sqrt[3]{125} \div \sqrt[3]{5} =$ a) _____   = b) $\sqrt{}$ = c) _____   d) _____
11. $\sqrt[5]{64} \div \sqrt[5]{2} =$ a) _____   = b) $\sqrt{}$ = c) _____   d) _____
12. $\sqrt[3]{x} \div \sqrt[3]{y} =$ a) _____   = b) $\sqrt{}$

Name: _____ Date: _____

PRIME FACTORS AND SIMPLIFYING SQUARE ROOT RADICALS

Problems involving **square root radicals** can be written in a **simplified** form to solve the problems more efficiently. First, it is important to determine the **prime factors of the radicand**.

> **Prime factors:** A *natural number* (1, 2, 3, 4, 5...) greater than 1 is *prime* if no number other than 1 and the number itself can divide the number and result in another whole number. A *prime number* has exactly two factors: the natural number 1 and the number itself.

When finding the prime factors of a number, begin by dividing the number by 2 or 3. Continue dividing by 2 or another **natural number** (1, 2, 3, 4, 5...) until the number left is divisible only by 1 or the number.

Example 1: Find prime factors for 24. $24 \div 2 = 12$ $12 \div 2 = 6$ $6 \div 2 = 3$ The prime factors for 24 are 2, 2, 2, and 3. $2 \cdot 2 \cdot 2 \cdot 3 = 24$ Note that 2 and 3 are divisible only by 1 and the numbers 2 or 3.

Example 2: Find the prime factors for 15. $15 \div 2$ does not equal a natural number. Try $15 \div 3 = 5$. Five is divisible only by 5 or 1. The prime numbers for 15 are **5** and **3**.

Example 3: Find the prime factors for 90. $90 \div 2 = 45$ $45 \div 3 = 15$ $15 \div 3 = 5$

Directions: Find the prime factors for each of the following numbers. List the prime factors on the blank.

1. 14 the prime factors are _____   **2.** 600 the prime factors are _____

3. 512 the prime factors are _____   **4.** 238 the prime factors are _____

When two similar square radicals are multiplied, the answer is that number itself.

Example 1: Find $\sqrt{4} \cdot \sqrt{4}$. $2 \cdot 2 = 4$ so $\sqrt{4} \cdot \sqrt{4} = 4$

Example 2: Find $\sqrt{2} \cdot \sqrt{2}$. $1.414213562 \cdot 1.414213562 = 2$ so $\sqrt{2} \cdot \sqrt{2} = 2$

Example 3: Find $2\sqrt{2} \cdot \sqrt{2}$. $2 \cdot 1.414213562 \cdot 1.414213562 = 4$ so $2\sqrt{2} \cdot \sqrt{2} = 4$

Now you can use what you know about prime factors to simplify square root radicals.

Example 4: Simplify $\sqrt{18}$. The prime factors are $2 \cdot 3 \cdot 3$, so $\sqrt{18}$ can be rewritten as $\sqrt{2} \cdot \sqrt{3} \cdot \sqrt{3}$.

Simplify $\sqrt{18}$. $\sqrt{2} \cdot \sqrt{3} \cdot \sqrt{3} = \sqrt{2} \cdot 3 = 3\sqrt{2} = 3 \cdot 1.414213542 = 4.242640686$
$\sqrt{18} = 4.242640686$

Directions: Simplify the following problem involving square root radicals.

5. $\sqrt{12} + \sqrt{18} =$ **a)** prime factors of 12 _____

   b) $\sqrt{12}$ simplified _____

   c) the prime factors of 18 _____

   d) $\sqrt{18}$ simplified _____

   e) The simplified $\sqrt{12} + \sqrt{18} =$ _____ + _____ = _____

Name: _____ Date: _____

RATIONALIZING THE DENOMINATORS IN RADICALS WITH FRACTIONS

In many problems, fractions and radicals will appear together. Many fractions with radicals can be simplified by finding the roots of the numerator and denominator.

Examples: $\dfrac{\sqrt{4}}{\sqrt{9}} = \dfrac{2}{3}$ or $\dfrac{\sqrt{16}}{\sqrt{49}} = \dfrac{4}{7}$

In the examples above, each of the roots resulted in a **rational number**. Many times the fraction under the radical contains a denominator that is an **irrational number**.

Example: In $\dfrac{\sqrt{4}}{\sqrt{7}}$, the square root of seven is an irrational number.

To **rationalize** the denominator, the fraction is changed so the denominator does not have a radical.

Example: To rationalize $\dfrac{\sqrt{4}}{\sqrt{7}}$, it is necessary to find a number that can be multiplied times $\sqrt{7}$ and result in a rational number. You have learned that $\sqrt{7} \cdot \sqrt{7} = 7$. Seven is a rational number. If the denominator is multiplied by $\sqrt{7}$, the numerator must be multiplied by $\sqrt{7}$.

To rationalize the denominator of $\dfrac{\sqrt{4}}{\sqrt{7}}$, the numerator and denominator must both be multiplied by $\sqrt{7}$.

$$\frac{\sqrt{4}}{\sqrt{7}} \cdot \frac{\sqrt{7}}{\sqrt{7}} = \frac{\sqrt{28}}{7}$$

A radical is in **simplified form** when the radicand has no roots other than 1. The radical $\dfrac{\sqrt{28}}{7}$ needs to be simplified because $\sqrt{28} = \sqrt{4} \cdot \sqrt{7}$. Seven has no roots other than 7 and 1. However, the root of 4 is 2.

Simplified: $\dfrac{\sqrt{28}}{7} = \sqrt{4} \cdot \dfrac{\sqrt{7}}{7} = \dfrac{2\sqrt{7}}{7}$

Directions: Simplify the following. Show all steps.

1. $\dfrac{\sqrt{4}}{\sqrt{5}} =$

2. $\dfrac{\sqrt{2}}{\sqrt{3}} =$

3. $\dfrac{\sqrt{3}}{\sqrt{6}} =$

4. $\dfrac{\sqrt{50}}{\sqrt{2}} =$

5. $\dfrac{\sqrt{8}}{\sqrt{2}} =$

Name: _____ Date: _____

LEARNING ABOUT RADICALS IN EQUATIONS

Radicals often occur in equations. An **equation** states that two numbers or algebraic expressions are equal. When a radical appears in an equation, a variable (unknown) appears as the radicand. **Variables** are letters, sometimes called literal numbers, used to represent numbers. Any letter *a* through *z* may be used as a variable.

Example: $\sqrt{x} = 2$ is an equation with a radical. The radicand is a variable (x).

To solve equations like $\sqrt{x} = 2$, use the following steps.

Step 1: Square each side of the equation: $\sqrt{x} \cdot \sqrt{x} = 2 \cdot 2$ results in $x = 4$
Step 2: Substitute 4 in the original equation and solve the equation.
$\sqrt{4} = 2$. The square root of 4 is 2.
Step 3: Rewrite the equation with 2 replacing $\sqrt{4}$. $2 = 2$

Directions: Solve the following. In blank a) show the radical side of the equation squared, in blank b) show the other side of the equation squared, in c) indicate what the variable equals, in d) rewrite the equation replacing the variable, and in e) rewrite the solved equation. The first one has been completed.

1. $\sqrt{x} = 3$ a) $\sqrt{x} \cdot \sqrt{x}$ b) $3 \cdot 3$ c) $x = 9$ d) $\sqrt{9} = 3$ e) $3 = 3$

2. $\sqrt{x} = 4$ a) _____   b) _____   c) _____   d) _____   e) _____

3. $\sqrt{x} = 9$ a) _____   b) _____   c) _____   d) _____   e) _____

4. $\sqrt{x} = 5$ a) _____   b) _____   c) _____   d) _____   e) _____

5. $\sqrt{x} = 6$ a) _____   b) _____   c) _____   d) _____   e) _____

6. $\sqrt{x} = 7$ a) _____   b) _____   c) _____   d) _____   e) _____

7. $\sqrt{x} = 8$ a) _____   b) _____   c) _____   d) _____   e) _____

8. $\sqrt{x} = 12$ a) _____   b) _____   c) _____   d) _____   e) _____

9. $\sqrt{x} = 15$ a) _____   b) _____   c) _____   d) _____   e) _____

10. $\sqrt{x} = 10$ a) _____   b) _____   c) _____   d) _____   e) _____

Name: _____ Date: _____

Quiz VII: Learning About Radicals and Roots

Directions: Complete the following exercises as directed.

Draw a radical for each of the following statements.

1. The square root of forty-nine. _____

2. The fourth root of sixty-four. _____

3. The cube root of one hundred twenty-five. _____

4. The eighth root of two hundred fifty-six. _____

Write the statement that expresses each of the following.

5. $\sqrt{8}$ _____

6. $\sqrt[3]{8}$ _____

7. $\sqrt[6]{78}$ _____

Find the indicated root of each radical and write the root on blank a). Write the factors on blank b).

8. $\sqrt{81}$ = a) _____ b) _____   **9.** $\sqrt[4]{16}$ = a) _____ b) _____

10. $\sqrt[3]{27}$ = a) _____ b) _____   **11.** $\sqrt[5]{32}$ = a) _____ b) _____

Multiply the following radicals.

12. $\sqrt{7} \cdot \sqrt{2}$ = _____   **13.** $\sqrt{7} \cdot \sqrt{5}$ = _____   **14.** $\sqrt{3} \cdot 2\sqrt{6}$ = _____

Divide the following.

15. $\sqrt{6} \div \sqrt{2}$ = _____   **16.** $\sqrt{24} \div \sqrt{8}$ = _____   **17.** $\sqrt{49} \div \sqrt{7}$ = _____

Simplify the following.

18. $\sqrt{12}$ = _____   **19.** $5\sqrt{18}$ = _____

20. $\dfrac{\sqrt{3}}{\sqrt{4}}$ = _____   **21.** $\dfrac{\sqrt{2}}{\sqrt{3}}$ = _____

Complete the following blanks.

22. Radicals can be added if the _____ and the _____ are the same.

23. Tell why the radicals $2\sqrt{12}$ and $3\sqrt{12}$ can be added. _____

24. Radicals can be subtracted if the _____ and the _____ are the same.

25. Tell why the radical $3\sqrt{12}$ cannot be subtracted from $2\sqrt{2}$. _____

_____

Name: _____ Date: _____

Learning About Linear Equations

Linear equations are **first-degree** equations. The graph of a linear equation is a straight line.

There are two requirements for an equation to be a first-degree equation.

1. In a first-degree equation, each of the **variables** has an exponent of 1.

    Example: x, y, and z all have exponents of 1, but x^2, y^3, z^4 all have exponents greater than 1.

2. Two variables do not appear as a **product** in any term.

    Example: x, y, and, z are individual variables, but xy, xz, and yz are examples of variables appearing as a product.
    If $x = 4$ and $y = 2$, then $xy = 4 \cdot 2 = 8$.

Examples: $x + y = 10$ The variables are x and y, and each have the exponent 1.
$3x - 2y = 11$ The variables are x and y, and each have the exponent 1.
$x^3 + y^2 = 17$ The variables x and y each have exponents greater than 1.

Examples: $x + y = 10$ The variables do not appear as a product in any term.
$2xy + 5 = 27$ The variables x and y appear as a product.
If $x = 4$ and $y = 3$, then $2xy + 5 = 29$ equals $2 \cdot 4 \cdot 3 + 5 = 29$

Directions: Place a (+) in front of each of the following that is a **first-degree** equation.

___ **1.** $xy = 36$ ___ **2.** $x - y = 7$ ___ **3.** $y = x + 14$ ___ **4.** $xy - z = 8$

___ **5.** $x + y - z = 10$ ___ **6.** $3x = 15$ ___ **7.** $2x + y = 15$ ___ **8.** $x^3 + y = 12$

___ **9.** $x + y^4 = 19$ ___ **10.** $xy - z^2 = 16$

Directions: Solve for the value of y if $x = 3$.

11. $y = x + 9$ $y = $ _____   **12.** $x - y = 14$ $y = $ _____

Directions: Solve for the value of x if $y = 6$.

13. $3x + y = 18$ $x = $ _____   **14.** $x = 12 - y$ $x = $ _____

Name: _____ Date: _____

DETERMINING THE SLOPE OF A GRAPHED LINEAR EQUATION

> Graphing linear equations always results in a straight line. If you locate the coordinates
> for two points and connect them with a straight line, the other coordinates that lie
> on the line will also be solutions to the equation.

The following coordinate system has graphs of the linear equations $y = 3x$, $y = x$, and
$y = -2x$.

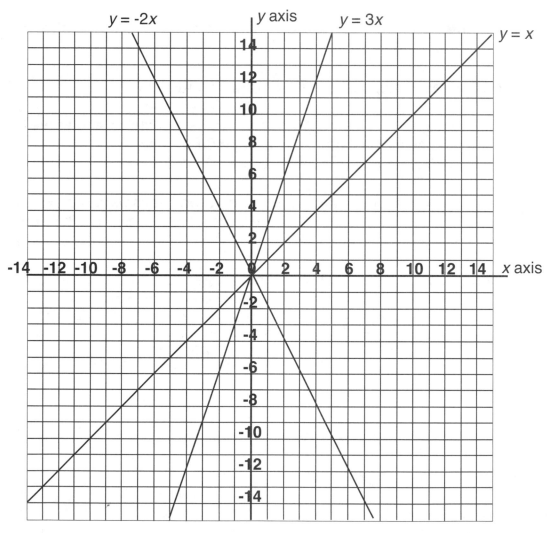

Fill in the following. Select your answers from: **linear; straight; first; x; y;** and **0,0**. Each is used
only once.

1. The graphs of all three equations are _____ lines.

2. All three of the equations are of the _____ degree.

3. All three of the equations are _____ equations.

4. All three graphs cross the "___" and "___" axes at the coordinates ___, ___.

Name: _____ Date: _____

DETERMINING THE SLOPE OF A GRAPHED LINEAR EQUATION
(CONTINUED)

The graph of a linear equation may be referred to as **positive** or **negative.** To determine if a graph is positive or negative, the **slope** of the graph must be determined. In determining the slope, the graph is read from left to right to determine if the graph slopes up or down. See "A" and "B" below.

A. Positive Slope

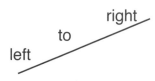

B. Negative Slope

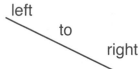

Graph A above is a positive-sloping graph since the line slopes up when read from left to right. Graph B is a negative-sloping graph since the line slopes down when read from left to right.

Directions: Answer the following questions.

5. The graph of the linear equation $y = 3x$ slopes _____ from left to _____ and is a _____-sloping graph.

6. The graph of the linear equation $y = x$ slopes _____ from _____ to right and is a _____-sloping graph.

7. The graph of the linear equation $y = -2x$ slopes _____ from _____ to right and is a _____-sloping graph.

Making a table of values for the x and y coordinates that are solutions to the equation is helpful. In making a table, numerical values are chosen and assigned to x. Then the equation is solved for y, and the numerical values are placed in table format.

Directions: Develop numerical values for the linear equations $y = 3x$ and $y = -3x$ and place the values in the tables below.

$y = 3x$

If $x =$				
Then $y =$				

$y = -3x$

If $x =$				
Then $y =$				

Name: _____ Date: _____

DETERMINING THE SLOPE OF A GRAPHED LINEAR EQUATION (CONTINUED)

Directions: Use the numerical values from the tables on the previous page to graph the equations $y = 3x$ and $y = -3x$ on the coordinate system below. For each pair of coordinates, the x coordinate is written first and the y coordinate is written second. Find the x coordinate on the grid by moving along the x axis. Then move up or down on the line of the x coordinate until you find the point where it intersects the line of the y coordinate. Mark that point with a dot and then continue to find the other points from the table. Connect the dots for each equation with a straight line.

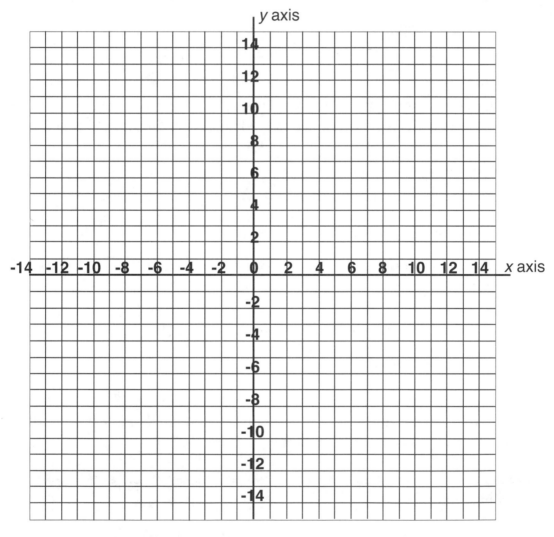

Directions: Answer the following questions.

8. The equation ___ = _____ is a positive-sloping graph because when read _____

_____

9. The equation ___ = _____ is a negative-sloping graph because when read _____

_____

Name: _____ Date: _____

POSITIVE AND NEGATIVE SLOPE

It is important to determine if the slope of a graph is **positive** or **negative** as well as how **steep** the slope of the line is. In order to determine how steep the slope of a line is, one needs to determine how much *y* changes with each change in *x*.

Directions: Refer to the graph of the linear equation $y = 3x$ on the coordinate system below. Answer the following questions.

1. In determining the slope of the line, one must read the line from **a)** right to left **b)** left to right.

2. The slope of the line $y = 3x$ is (up/down).

3. The slope of the line is (negative/positive).

You will note that the graph of $y = 3x$ on the coordinate system below has dashed lines (- -) marked a–f. Refer to this dashed line and answer the following questions.

4. In moving from "a" to "b," one moves **a)** 1 **b)** 2 **c)** 3 **d)** 4 places on the *x* line.

5. In moving from "b" to "c," one moves **a)** 1 **b)** 2 **c)** 3 **d)** 4 places on the *y* line.

6. In moving from "c" to "d," one moves **a)** 1 **b)** 2 **c)** 3 **d)** 4 places on the *x* line.

7. In moving from "d" to "e," one moves **a)** 1 **b)** 2 **c)** 3 **d)** 4 places on the *y* line.

8. In moving from "e" to "f," one moves **a)** 1 **b)** 2 **c)** 3 **d)** 4 places on the *x* line.

9. In the graph of $y = 3x$, each time the *x* position changed by **a)** 1 **b)** 2 **c)** 3 **d)** 4.

10. In the graph of $y = 3x$, each time the *y* position changed by **a)** 1 **b)** 2 **c)** 3 **d)** 4.

11. In the graph of $y = 3x$, the change in *y* is **a)** 3 **b)** 1 **c)** 5 **d)** 10 times the change in *x*.

12. In the graph of $y = 3x$, the change in *x* is **a)** 1/5 **b)** 1/3 **c)** 1/10 **d)** 1/100 of the change in *y*.

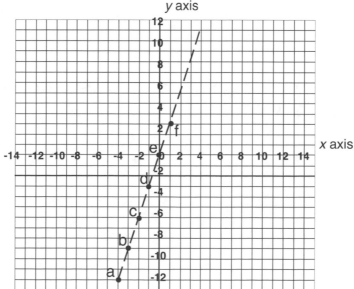

Name: _____ Date: _____

FORMULA FOR DETERMINING THE SLOPE OF A GRAPHED LINEAR EQUATION

The following formula is used in determining the slope of the graph of a linear equation.

$$\text{Slope} = \frac{y_2 - y_1}{x_2 - x_1}$$

The solution of the equation requires any two y (y_2, y_1) coordinates and any two x (x_2, x_1) coordinates from the same sets of coordinates or graph.

The following coordinates for the linear equation $y = 3x$ can be used to demonstrate the above formula. The coordinates are (1,3) (2,6) (0,0) (-1,-3). Remember the first number in each set of coordinates is the x coordinate, and the second number in the set is the y coordinate.

Example: Use the formula $\text{Slope} = \dfrac{y_2 - y_1}{x_2 - x_1}$

and the above coordinates of the graph $y = 3x$ to find the slope of the graph. Substitute the coordinates sets of (1,3) and (2,6) in the above formula to determine the slope of the linear equation $y = 3x$.

$$\text{Slope} = \frac{6 - 3}{2 - 1} = \frac{3}{1} = 3 \quad \text{The slope of the linear equation } y = 3x \text{ is 3.}$$

Directions: Refer again to the graph of the equation $y = 3x$ on page 50 and complete the following exercise.

1. Place a plus (+) by the sets of coordinates that lie on the graph for the linear equation $y = 3x$.

  ___ **a)** 3,9   ___ **b)** 2,2   ___ **c)** -2,-6   ___ **d)** 7,21

  ___ **e)** -4,-12   ___ **f)** 5,15

2. Plot the coordinates for Question 1 that lie on the graph $y = 3x$, and draw a line connecting the coordinates on the graph.

Name: _____ Date: _____

GRAPHING LINEAR EQUATIONS AND DETERMINING THEIR SLOPES

Directions: Determine a table of values for the following linear equations and plot the points on the coordinate system below. Draw lines to graph the sets of coordinates.

1. $y = 2x + 1$

If $x =$						
Then $y =$						

2. $y = 2x - 1$

If $x =$						
Then $y =$						

3. $y = -2x + 1$

If $x =$						
Then $y =$						

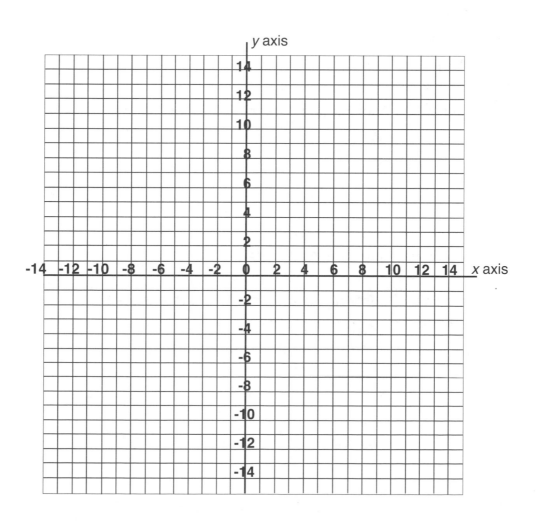

Name: _____ Date: _____

GRAPHING LINEAR EQUATIONS AND DETERMINING THEIR SLOPES (CONTINUED)

Directions: Refer to the graphs for $y = 2x + 1$, $y = 2x - 1$, and $y = -2x + 1$, and answer the following questions.

Linear equation $y = 2x + 1$

4. The slope of the linear equation $y = 2x + 1$ is (negative/positive).

5. Coordinates for the linear equation $y = 2x + 1$ are _____, _____, _____, _____, _____.

6. Choose four sets of two coordinates for $y = 2x + 1$ and complete the formula below. Determine the slope of the graph.

Slope = ——— = —— =   Slope = ——— = —— =

Slope = ——— = —— =   Slope = ——— = —— =

7. The slope of the linear equation $y = 2x + 1$ is _____.

Linear equation $y = 2x - 1$

8. The slope of the linear equation $y = 2x - 1$ is (negative/positive).

9. Coordinates for the linear equation $y = 2x - 1$ are _____, _____, _____, _____, _____.

10. Complete the following formulas and determine the steepness of the slope.

Slope = ——— = —— =   Slope = ——— = —— =

Slope = ——— = —— =   Slope = ——— = —— =

11. The slope of the linear equation $y = 2x - 1$ is _____.

Linear equation $y = -2x + 1$

12. The slope of the linear equation $y = -2x + 1$ is (negative/positive).

13. Coordinates for the linear equation $y = -2x + 1$ are _____, _____, _____, _____, _____.

14. Complete the following formulas and determine the steepness of the slope.

Slope = ——— = —— =   Slope = ——— = —— =

Slope = ——— = —— =   Slope = ——— = —— =

15. The slope of the linear equation $y = -2x + 1$ is _____.

Name: _____ Date: _____

LEARNING ABOUT THE *x*-INTERCEPT AND THE *y*-INTERCEPT

The coordinates where the graph of a linear equation crosses the *x* axis and *y* axis are important coordinates. In algebra, these coordinates are known as the *x*-intercept and *y*-intercept.

Directions: To begin learning about the *x*- and *y*-intercepts, graph the following linear equations on the coordinate system below. Plot the coordinates following each equation.

A. $y = 3x + 2$ (0,2) (-1,-1) (1,5)

B. $y = 3x - 2$ (0,-2) (2,4) (-1,-5)

C. $y = x + 5$ (0,5) (-5,0) (3,8)

D. $y = -x - 5$ (0,-5) (-5,0) (-8,3)

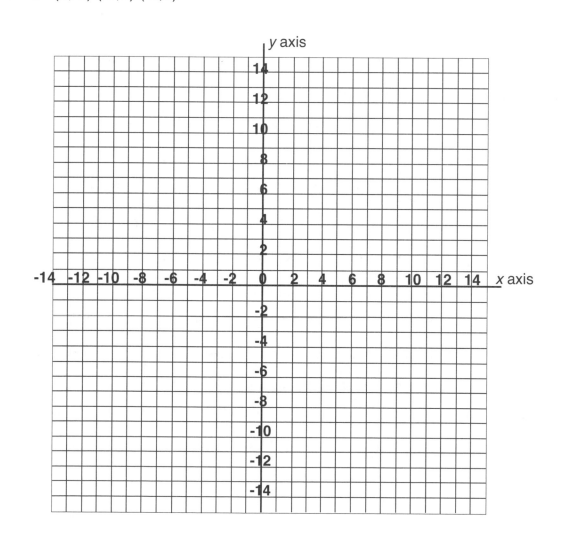

Name: _____ Date: _____

LEARNING ABOUT THE X-INTERCEPT AND THE Y-INTERCEPT (CONTINUED)

Directions: Refer to the graphs on the previous page and answer the following questions.

1. List the linear equations for the graph(s) with a positive slope.

_____

2. List the linear equations for the graph(s) with a negative slope.

_____

3. The linear equation $y = 3x + 2$ crosses the y-axis at the **coordinates** ___, ___.

4. The point where the graph of $y = 3x + 2$ crosses the y-axis is the **y-intercept**.

The **coordinates** for the y-intercept are ___, ___.

5. The point where the graph of $y = 3x + 2$ crosses the x-axis is the **x-intercept**.

The **coordinates** for the x-intercept are ___, ___.

6. The linear equation $y = 3x + 2$ crosses the x-axis at the **coordinates** ___, ___.

7. The coordinates for the **x-intercept** for the linear equation $y = 3x - 2$ are ___, ___.

8. The coordinates for the **y-intercept** for the linear equation $y = 3x - 2$ are ___, ___.

9. The coordinates for the **x-intercept** for the linear equation $y = x + 5$ are ___, ___.

10. The coordinates for the **y-intercept** for the linear equation $y = x + 5$ are ___, ___.

11. The coordinates for the **x-intercept** for the linear equation $y = -x - 5$ are ___, ___.

12. The coordinates for the **y-intercept** for the linear equation $y = -x - 5$ are ___, ___.

13. In locating the **x-intercept**, the y coordinate will always be   **a)** 6   **b)** 10   **c)** 0   **d)** 9.

14. In locating the **y-intercept**, the x coordinate will always be   **a)** 6   **b)** 10   **c)** 0   **d)** 9.

Directions: Solve the following equations

15. $y = 4x - 4$ (let x equal zero) $y = 4(\_\_\_) - 4$ $y = \_\_\_\_ = y$-intercept

16. $y = 4x - 4$ (let y equal zero) $0 = 4(\_\_\_) - 4$ $x = \_\_\_\_ = x$-intercept

17. $y = x + 2$ (let x equal zero) $y = (\_\_\_) + 2$ $y = \_\_\_\_ = y$-intercept

18. $y = x + 2$ (let y equal zero) $0 = (\_\_\_) + 2$ $x = \_\_\_\_ = x$-intercept

19. In solving the above equations to find the y-intercept, x equals ___.

20. In solving the above equations to find the x-intercept, y equals ___.

LEARNING ABOUT THE SLOPE-INTERCEPT EQUATION

Graphing linear equations to find the solution to an equation is an important problem-solving method. The equation $y = mx + b$ is valuable in the study of mathematics. This equation is called the **slope intercept equation**. To find the slope and y-intercept of a linear equation, the equation must be written in the form $y = mx + b$. It is important to note that the **slope** is the **ratio** of **vertical change** compared to the **horizontal change** in the graph.

> In solving linear equations using the slope-intercept equation, it is often necessary to rewrite the equation so that it is in the form $y = mx + b$.

Example: Rewrite the equation $3x - y = 8$ so that it is in the form $y = mx + b$.
Step 1: Add $(+y)$ to each member: $3x - y + y = 8 + y$ equals $3x = 8 + y$
Step 2: Subtract (-8) from each member: $3x - 8 = -8 + 8 + y$ equals $3x - 8 = y$
Step 3: $3x - 8 = y$ can be rewritten in the $y = mx + b$ form as $y = 3x - 8$
$y = 3x - 8$ is in the slope-intercept form
Step 4: Develop a table of values for the equation.
For example:

x	-2	-1	1	2	3	4
y	-14	-11	-5	-2	1	4

Step 5: Plot the graph for the coordinates in step 4.

The next exercise will help determine the slope of the equation $3x - y = 8$, which can be rewritten in the form $y = mx + b$ as $y = 3x - 8$. You will recall that the slope is the ratio of the vertical change in the graph compared to the horizontal change in the graph.

Directions: Use a colored pencil and complete the following on the graph on the next page.

1. Place a dot locating the coordinates (-2,-14).
2. Place a dot locating the coordinates (-1,-11).
3. On the x line draw a **horizontal** line from -2 to -1.
4. On the y line draw a **vertical** line from -14 to -11.
5. The **horizontal** line change is   **a)** 5   **b)** 6   **c)** 1   **d)** 9   unit(s).
6. The **vertical** line change is   **a)** 3   **b)** 8   **c)** 7   **d)** 6   units.
7. The ratio of vertical change to horizontal is   **a)** 3/1   **b)** 4/1   **c)** 5/1   **d)** 6/1.
8. Place a dot locating the coordinates (1,-5).
9. Place a dot locating the coordinates (2,-2).
10. On the x line draw a **horizontal** line from 1 to 2.
11. On the y line draw a **vertical** line from -5 to -2.
12. The **horizontal** line change is   **a)** 1   **b)** 5   **c)** 6   **d)** 9   unit(s).
13. The **vertical** line change is   **a)** 7   **b)** 8   **c)** 3   **d)** 6   units.
14. The ratio of vertical change to horizontal is   **a)** 4/1   **b)** 5/1   **c)** 3/1   **d)** 6/1.

Name: _____ Date: _____

LEARNING ABOUT THE SLOPE-INTERCEPT EQUATION (CONTINUED)

15. Place a dot locating the coordinates (3,1).

16. Place a dot locating the coordinates (4,4).

17. On the *x* line draw a **horizontal** line from 3 to 4.

18. On the *y* line draw a **vertical** line from 1 to 4.

19. The **horizontal** line change is   **a)** 9   **b)** 5   **c)** 6   **d)** 1   unit(s).

20. The **vertical** line change is   **a)** 7   **b)** 3   **c)** 8   **d)** 6   units.

21. The ratio of vertical change to horizontal is   **a)** 4/1   **b)** 6/1   **c)** 5/1   **d)** 3/1.

22. In the linear equation $y = 3x - 8$, the ratio of vertical change to horizontal change is

   ___ / ___ or ___.

Directions: Compare the equations $y = 3x - 8$ and $y = mx + b$ and answer the following questions.

23. In the equation $y = 3x - 8$, the number ___ replaces "*m*."

24. In the equation $y = 3x - 8$, the number ___ replaces "*b*."

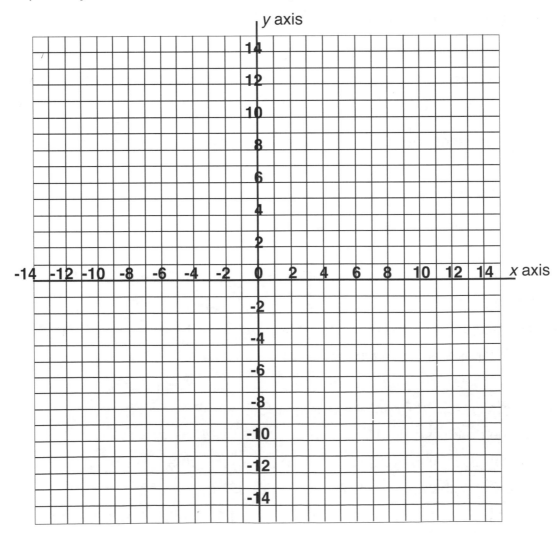

Name: _____ Date: _____

SLOPE-INTERCEPT EXERCISES

In the slope-intercept equation $y = mx + b$, the number replacing the letter m will always give the **slope** of the equation. The number that replaces the letter b will always be the **y-intercept**. Therefore, it is important to write a linear equation in the form $y = mx + b$.

Directions: Complete the following exercises as directed.

Write the following equations in the slope-intercept form.

1. $y - 1 = 2x$ _____

2. $y - 2x = 8$ _____

3. $y - 7 = x$ _____

4. $3y - x = 2$ _____

Give the slope and y-intercept for each of the following linear equations

5. $y = 4x + 5$ **a)** slope ___ / ___   **b)** y-intercept _____

6. $y = \frac{1}{2}x - 2$ **a)** slope ___ / ___   **b)** y-intercept _____

7. $y = x + 1$ **a)** slope ___ / ___   **b)** y-intercept _____

8. $y - 1 = x$ **a)** slope ___ / ___   **b)** y-intercept _____

Refer to the **slope-intercept equation** $y = mx + b$, and place a plus (+) by the true statements.

_____ **9.** In the slope-intercept equation, m indicates the slope of the line.

_____ **10.** In the slope-intercept equation, b locates the y-intercept.

_____ **11.** In the slope-intercept equation, y is the independent variable.

_____ **12.** In the slope-intercept equation, x is the dependent variable.

Refer to the graph below and answer the following questions.

13. The graph intercepts (crosses) the y-axis at   **a)** +9   **b)** +8   **c)** +1   **d)** +5.

14. The graph has a (negative/positive) slope.

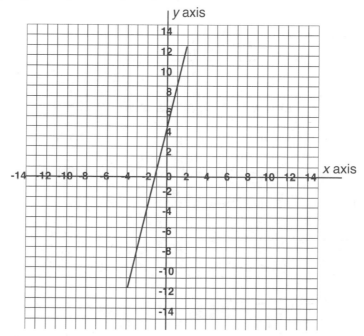

Name: _____ Date: _____

GRAPHING LINEAR EQUATIONS

Directions: In the next exercise, you will graph two linear equations on the same coordinate plane. Find two sets of coordinates that are solutions for each of the linear equations, locate the coordinates, and draw a graph of each linear equation.

Graph the linear equations $x + y = 8$ and $x - y = 4$.

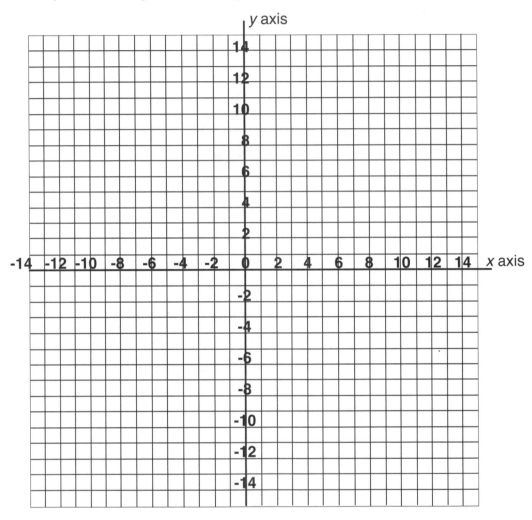

Refer to the graphs of $x + y = 8$ and $x - y = 4$, and answer the following questions.

1. The coordinates where the graphs cross are   **a)** 5,1   **b)** 6,2   **c)** -3,0   **d)** 6,8.

2. Substitute the coordinates where the graphs cross into each of the equations

   $x + y = 8$ and $x - y = 4$, and solve the equations.

   a) $x + y = 8$ _____   **b)** $x - y = 4$ _____

3. The coordinates **a)** (___, ___) where the graphs cross are solutions for both

   b) ___ + ___ = 8 and **c)** ___ - ___ = 4.

Name: _____ Date: _____

Quiz VIII: Learning About Linear Equations

Directions: Fill in the following blanks. Select answers from the list below. Each term may be used more than once.

positive	horizontal	one	linear equation	$y = mx + b$	down
vertical	left	negative	right	up	b
$y = 2x + 4$	ten	$y = -2x + 4$	m	numerator	two
denominator					

An equation in the form $y = 3x - 8$ is known as a **1.** _____ _____. The variables in a linear equation all have an exponent of **2.** _____. When a linear equation is graphed, the slope of the graph may be **3.** _____ or **4.** _____. The graph of a positive-sloping linear equation slopes **5.** _____ from left to right. The graph of a negative-sloping linear equation slopes **6.** _____ from left to right.

The graph of the linear equation **7.** ___ = ___ + ___ will slope down. It is a **8.** _____-sloping graph. The graph of the linear equation **9.** ___ = ___ + ___ will slope up. It is a **10.** _____-sloping graph.

The slope-intercept equation is **11.** ___ = ___ + ___. In the slope-intercept equation, the number replacing the letter **12.** ___ will always indicate the slope. The number replacing the letter **13.** ___ will be the *y*-intercept. The slope of a graph is the ratio of the **14.** _____ change compared to the **15.** _____ change. The ratio of the slope is written as a fraction with the **16.** _____ indicating the vertical change and the **17.** _____ indicating the horizontal change. The *y*-intercept of the graph for the linear equation $y = 2x + 10$ is **18.** _____. The slope of the graph for the linear equation $y = 2x + 10$ is **19.** _____.

Name: _____ Date: _____

Learning About Quadratic Equations

The **quadratic equation** is one of the most important algebraic tools. It is a second-degree polynomial with one variable (unknown). In standard form, a quadratic equation is written as $ax^2 + bx + c = 0$.

In the form $ax^2 + bx + c = 0$, the equation is written in descending power for the variable x. To arrange in descending power of a variable, an equation is written from left to right with the variable descending in power.

Example: Arrange $x^3 + x^4 + (-2x) + 4x^5y$ in descending power of x.

The term with x^5 is the highest power, so $4x^5y$ is the first term. The term with the second highest power is x^4, the third term is x^3, and so forth. Arranged in order from highest to lowest power in the variable x, $x^3 + x^4 + (-2x) + 4x^5y$ becomes $4x^5y + x^4 + x^3 + (-2x)$.

Directions: Arrange the following in order from highest to lowest power for the variable indicated in parentheses.

1. $x^2 + x^5 + x^3 - y$ $(x) =$ ____ + ____ + ____ - ____

2. $a^3 - a^2 + a^4$ $(a) =$ ____ + ____ - ____

3. $5xy^3 - 4y^4 + y^2 - 2$ $(y) =$ _____

4. $5b^2 + b^4 - b^3 + 10b$ $(b) =$ _____

5. $x + x^2 - y$ $(x) =$ _____

6. $7t^2y^5 - t^4 + t^3x^2 + a^3t$ $(t) =$ _____

7. $q^3x^2 + 9q + 4y^5q^8$ $(q) =$ _____

8. $-2d + 6d^2r + d^9g^4$ $(d) =$ _____

9. $3r^5t - 4ar - 2a^4r^2 + r^8x$ $(r) =$ _____

10. $y^2x^4 + 6yt^2 + 2y - 8y^3b^2$ $(y) =$ _____

GRAPHING THE EQUATION $AX^2 + BX + C$

You have learned that the graph of a linear equation is a straight line. In learning about the graphs of quadratics, we will begin with $y = ax^2$. In the following activities, you will graph sets of quadratic coordinates. You will find that each of the graphs results in a form known as a **parabola**. After graphing the different quadratics, you will be asked to determine one of the important characteristics of the parabola.

Directions: Graph the four equations shown below. Your teacher will give you two copies of the coordinate system on page 63. Place graph 1 and 2 on one coordinate system and graphs 3 and 4 on the other coordinate system.

Graph 1: $y = 1x^2$ The table of values is below. In this example $a = 1$.

x	0	1	2	3	-1	-2	-3
y	0	1	4	9	1	4	9

The coordinates of the graph will be (0,0), (1,1), (2,4), (3,9), (-1,1), (-2,4), and (-3,9). Plot the coordinates of the graph of $y = ax^2$ on the coordinate system on page 63. Connect the coordinates with a line.

Graph 2: $y = -2x^2$. The table of values is below. In this example $a = -2$.

x	0	1	2	3	-1	-2	-3
y	0	-2	-8	-18	-2	-8	-18

The coordinates of the graph will be (0,0), (1,-2), (2,-8), (3,-18), (-1,-2), (-2,-8), and (-3,-18). Plot the graph on the coordinate system and connect the coordinates with a line.

Graph 3: $x = 1y^2$. The table of values is below. $a = 1$

y	0	1	2	3	-1	-2	-3
x	0	1	4	9	1	4	9

Plot the graph of $x = 1y^2$ on the coordinate system and connect the coordinates with a line.

Graph 4: $x = -2y^2$ The table of values is below. $a = -2$

y	0	1	2	3	-1	-2	-3
x	0	-2	-8	-18	-2	-8	-18

Plot the graph of $x = -2y^2$ on the coordinate system and connect the coordinates with a line.

Name: _____ Date: _____

GRAPHING THE EQUATION $AX^2 + BX + C$ (CONTINUED)

Directions: Graph the quadratic equations from the previous page on the coordinate system below.

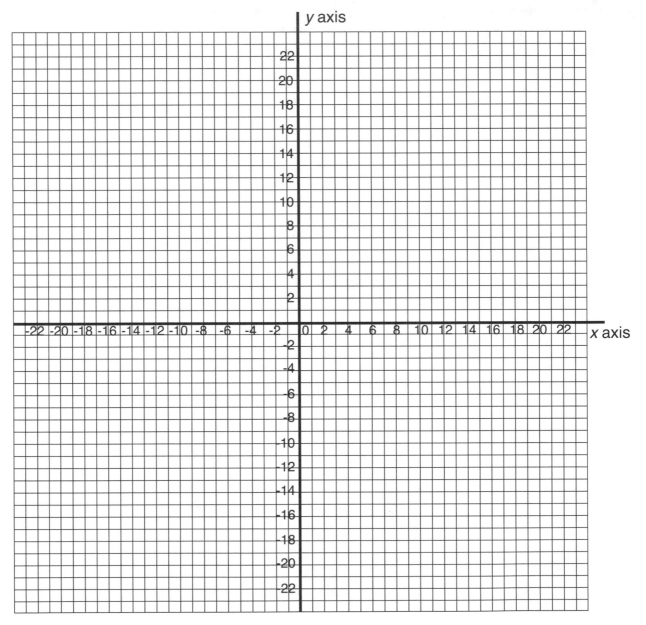

Name: _____ Date: _____

PARABOLAS

Each of the graphs you have drawn on page 63 is a **parabola**. In the study of parabolas, the terms **vertex**, **minimum coordinates**, and **maximum coordinates** are very important.

Directions: Below you will find two parabolas marked "A" and "B". Use these parabolas to answer the following questions.

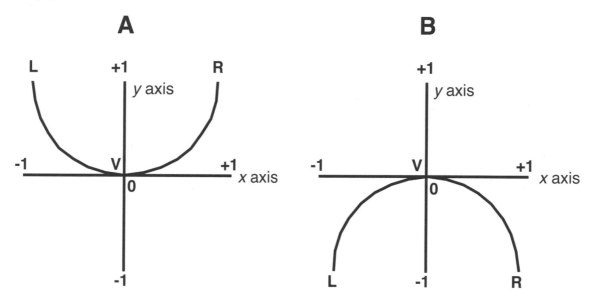

Refer to Parabola A and answer the following questions. Begin at Point **L** and follow the curve of the parabola to Point **V**.

1. The change in "y" as you move down the curve from Point L to Point V is from

   + ___ to ___.

2. From Point L to Point V the value of "y" is (decreasing/increasing).

3. The change in "x" as you move down the curve from Point L to Point V is from

   - ___ to ___.

4. From Point L to Point V the value of "x" is (decreasing/increasing).

Refer to Parabola A and answer the following questions. Begin at Point **R** and follow the curve of the parabola to Point **V**.

5. The change in "y" as you move down the curve from Point R to Point V is from

   + ___ to ___.

6. From Point R to Point V the value of "y" is (decreasing/increasing).

7. The change in "x" as you move down the curve from Point R to Point V is from

   + ___ to ___.

8. From Point R to Point V the value of "x" is (decreasing/increasing).

Name: _____ Date: _____

PARABOLAS (CONTINUED)

Complete the following blanks using these terms: **maximum, minimum, vertex.**

On Parabola A, the coordinates of "*x*" and "*y*" reach their largest or **9.** _____

values at Points L and R. The coordinates of "*x*" and "*y*" reach their smallest or

10. _____ values at Point V. Point V is the **11.** _____ value for

Parabola A.

Refer to Parabola B on the previous page and answer the following questions. Begin at Point **L** and follow the curve on the parabola to Point **V**.

12. The change in "*y*" as you move up the curve from Point L to Point V is from - ___ to ___.

13. From Point L to Point V the value of "*y*" is (decreasing/increasing).

14. The change in "*x*" as you move up the curve from Point L to Point V is from - ___ to ___.

15. From Point L to Point V the value of "*x*" is (decreasing/increasing).

Refer to Parabola B and answer the following questions. Begin at Point **R** and follow the curve on the parabola to Point **V**.

16. The change in "*y*" as you move up the curve from Point R to Point V is from - ___ to ___.

17. From Point R to Point V the value of "*y*" is (decreasing/increasing).

18. The change in "*x*" as you move up the curve from Point R to Point V is from + ___ to ___.

19. From Point R to Point V the value of "*x*" is (decreasing/increasing).

Complete the following blanks using the following terms: **maximum, minimum, vertex.**

On Parabola B, the coordinates of "*x*" and "*y*" reach their largest or **20.** _____

values at Point V. The coordinates of "*x*" and "*y*" reach their smallest or **21.** _____

values at Points L and R. Point V is the **22.** _____ value for Parabola B.

PARABOLA PRACTICE

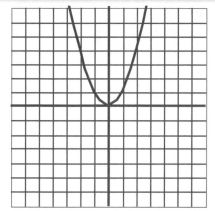

$y = ax^2$

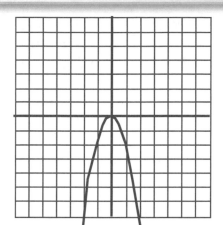

$y = -2x^2$

Directions: Refer to the parabola for $y = ax^2$, follow the instructions below, and answer the questions.

1. The minimum coordinates for the graph are **a)** 0,0 **b)** -1,-2 **c)** 1,1 **d)** -2,-2

2. Draw a line from (-1,1) through (0,1) to (1,1)

3. From (-1,1) to (0,1), the line is drawn through **a)** 1 **b)** 4 **c)** 7 **d)** 0 rectangles.

4. From (0,1) to (1,1), the line is drawn through **a)** 1 **b)** 4 **c)** 7 **d)** 0 rectangles.

5. Draw a line from (-2,3) through (0,3) to (2,3)

6. From (-2,3) to (0,3), the line is drawn through **a)** 1 **b)** 2 **c)** 3 **d)** 0 rectangles.

7. From (0,3) to (2,3), the line is drawn through **a)** 1 **b)** 2 **c)** 3 **d)** 0 rectangles.

Directions: Refer to the parabola for $y = -2x^2$, follow the instructions below, and answer the questions.

8. The maximum coordinates for the graph are **a)** 0,0 **b)** -1,-2 **c)** 1,1 **d)** -2,-2

9. Carefully fold the graphs for $y = ax^2$ and $y = -2x^2$ along the "y" axis.

10. Carefully fold the graphs for $x = ay^2$ and $x = -2y^2$ along the "x" axis.

11. When folded, the left and right sides of the graphs match exactly. (true/false)

12. The ("x"/ "y") axis divides the parabolas in #9 above into two equal halves.

13. Define the word *symmetric:* _____

Directions: Complete the following: Use the following terms.

$y = ax^2$ $y = -2x^2$ **symmetric** **y axis** **parabola** **(0,0)**

The graphs for $y = ax^2$ and $y = -2x^2$ are **14.** _____. Each of the graphs is a

15. _____. The graph of **16.** $y =$ ___ reaches its minimum point at the vertex. The

graph of **17.** $y =$ ___ reaches its maximum point at the vertex. In both graphs the vertex

coordinates are **18.** (___, ___)

Name: _____ Date: _____

SOLVING QUADRATIC EQUATIONS

The quadratic equation is in **standard form** when it is in the form $ax^2 + bx + c = y$. In solving equations, numbers will often replace the letters a, b, and c in the equation. For example: $2x^2 + 3x + 4 = y$; $-4x^2 + 8x + 1 = y$; and so forth.

> **Examples:** Solve $2x^2 + 3x + 4 = y$ if $x = 2$. The equation becomes $2 \cdot 2^2 + 3 \cdot 2 + 4 = y$, which becomes $8 + 6 + 4 = 18$.
> Solve $-4x^2 + 8x + 1 = y$ if $x = 3$. The equation becomes $-4 \cdot 3^2 + 8 \cdot 3 + 1 = y$, which becomes $-36 + 24 + 1 = -11$.

Directions: Solve the following. The first one is completed.

1. $ax^2 + bx + c = y$ ($x = 2$, $a = 1$, $b = 3$, $c = 1$)   a) $1 \cdot 2^2 + 3 \cdot 2 + 1 = y$

   b) $4 + 6 + 1 = 11$ c) $11 = 11$

2. $-3x^2 + 4x + 4 = y$ ($x = 3$) a) _____ b) _____ c) _____

3. $ax^2 + bx + c = y$ ($x = -3$, $a = -1$, $b = 3$, $c = 1$) a) _____

   b) _____ c) _____

4. $ax^2 + bx + c = y$ ($x = 2$, $a = -4$, $b = 3$, $c = 1$) a) _____

   b) _____ c) _____

5. $ax^2 + bx + c = y$ ($x = -2$, $a = -1$, $b = 3$, $c = 1$) a) _____

   b) _____ c) _____

6. $2x^2 + 3x - 1 = y$ ($x = \frac{1}{2}$) a) _____ b) _____ c) _____

In many cases, the quadratic will not be in the **standard form** of $ax^2 + bx + c = y$.

> **Example:** $x^2 - 6x = -8$ is not in standard form. It is placed in standard form by adding +8 to each side of the equation. The equation is then written as $x^2 - 6x + 8 = -8 + 8$. The equation is then rewritten in standard form as $x^2 - 6x + 8 = 0$.

Directions: Rewrite each of the following in standard form. The first one has been completed.

7. $x^2 + 8x = -16$ a) $x^2 + 8x + 16 = -16 + 16$ b) $x^2 + 8x + 16 = 0$

8. $x^2 - 7x = -6$ a) _____   b) _____

9. $4x^2 - 16x = 20$ a) _____   b) _____

10. $10x^2 + 6x = 2$ a) _____   b) _____

11. $11x^2 + 3x = -4$ a) _____   b) _____

Name: _____ Date: _____

SOLVING QUADRATICS BY FACTORING

There are several methods for solving quadratic equations. Two of the methods are (1) factoring and (2) using the quadratic formula.

Factoring: A quadratic is the product of two binomials. In factoring a quadratic, you are finding the two binomials. x is a member of each binomial.

Example: Factor $x^2 - 4x + 4 = 0$
  Step 1: Set up two binomials with x as the first member of each $(x - ?)(x - ?)$.
  Step 2: Find two numbers that if added will equal $-4x$ and if multiplied will equal $+4$.

$$x^2 - 4x + 4 = (x - 2)(x - 2) = \begin{array}{r} x - 2 \\ \underline{x - 2} \\ x^2 - 2x \\ \underline{-2x + 4} \\ x^2 - 4x + 4 \end{array}$$

Once the equation is factored into $(x - 2)(x - 2)$, it is important to determine the number that must be substituted for "x" so that $(x - 2)(x - 2)$ equals zero. In this case if "x" equals $+2$ it will result in the problem $2 - 2$, which is equal to zero. Therefore, $(x - 2)(x - 2)$ equals zero.

Directions: Each of the following quadratics can be solved by factoring. Find the factors and solve the equation. The first one has been completed. Remember **not all quadratics can be solved by factoring.**

1. $x^2 + 4x - 12 = 0$ a) $(x + 6)(x - 2)$ b) $x = -6$ or $x = 2$

2. $x^2 - 6x + 9 = 0$ a) _____ b) _____

3. $x^2 + 5x + 6 = 0$ a) _____ b) _____

4. $x^2 - 10x + 24 = 0$ a) _____ b) _____

5. $x^2 - 7x + 12 = 0$ a) _____ b) _____

6. $x^2 + 8x + 16 = 0$ a) _____ b) _____

7. $x^2 - 2x + 1 = 0$ a) _____ b) _____

8. $x^2 - 7x + 10 = 0$ a) _____ b) _____

9. $x^2 + 3x + 2 = 0$ a) _____ b) _____

10. $y^2 + 2y - 3 = 0$ a) _____ b) _____

Name: _____ Date: _____

SOLVING QUADRATICS BY THE QUADRATIC FORMULA

The solution to any quadratic equation can be found using the quadratic formula. You will study the development of the quadratic formula and why it works in your study of algebra. The purpose of this exercise is to introduce the quadratic formula and provide some exercises in how it can be used.

The **quadratic formula** is $x = \dfrac{-b \pm \sqrt{b^2 - 4ac}}{2a}$

Example: Solve $x^2 - 4x - 5 = 0$ using the formula.

In using the formula, it is important to think of the quadratic equation in standard form $ax^2 + bx + c = 0$. $x^2 - 4x - 5 = 0$ is in standard form.

When the equation $x^2 - 4x - 5 = 0$ is in standard form, $a = 1$, $b = -4$, and $c = -5$. Now to solve the equation $x^2 - 4x - 5 = 0$ using the formula, the numbers for a, b, and c must be substituted in the equation.

The quadratic formula $x = \dfrac{-b \pm \sqrt{b^2 - 4ac}}{2a}$ becomes $x = \dfrac{-(-4) \pm \sqrt{(-4)^2 - 4(1)(-5)}}{2(1)}$

becomes $x = \dfrac{-(-4) \pm \sqrt{16 + 20}}{2}$ becomes $x = \dfrac{4 \pm \sqrt{36}}{2}$ becomes $x = \dfrac{4 \pm 6}{2}$

becomes $x = 5$ or $x = -1$.

Now $x = 5$ or $x = -1$. To determine if $x = 5$ or $x = -1$ is the correct solution to the quadratic, each must be substituted into the equation $x^2 - 4x - 5 = 0$.

$$x = -1 \qquad (-1)^2 - 4(-1) - 5 = 0 \qquad -1 \text{ is a solution}$$
$$x = 5 \qquad 5^2 - 4(5) - 5 = 0 \qquad +5 \text{ is a solution}$$

Directions: Solve the following. Substitute the numbers for a, b, and c in the formula, and determine the possible solutions for x. Then substitute each possible solution into the equation, and determine the solution. Show all the steps you take in solving the equation. The first one has been completed.

1. $x^2 + 6x - 16 = 0 \qquad\qquad a = 1, b = 6, c = -16$

$$x = \frac{-b \pm \sqrt{b^2 - 4ac}}{2a} = \frac{-(+6) \pm \sqrt{(6)^2 - 4(1)(-16)}}{2(1)} = \frac{-6 \pm \sqrt{36 + 64}}{2(1)} = \frac{-6 \pm \sqrt{100}}{2(1)} =$$

$$\frac{-6 + 10}{2} = \frac{+4}{2} = +2 \quad \text{or} \quad \frac{-6 - 10}{2} = \frac{-16}{2} = -8$$

Possible solutions to the equation
+2 and -8

Check: $x^2 + 6x - 16 = 0 = (2)^2 + 6(2) - 16 = 0$
Check: $x^2 + 6x - 16 = 0 = (-8)^2 + 6(-8) - 16 = 0$ Solution: +2, -8

SOLVING QUADRATICS BY THE QUADRATIC FORMULA (CONTINUED)

2. $x^2 - 2x - 8 = 0$ $a = 1$ $b = -2$ $c = -8$

Possible solutions to equation: _____   _____

Check: _____

Solution: _____

3. $x^2 - 2x - 4 = 0$ $a = 1$ $b = -2$ $c = -4$

Possible solutions to equation: _____   _____

Check: _____

Solution: _____

4. $x^2 + 2x - 1 = 0$ $a = 1$ $b = 2$ $c = -1$

Possible solutions to equation: _____   _____

Check: _____

Solution: _____

5. $2x^2 + x - 5 = 0$ $a = 2$ $b = 1$ $c = -5$

Possible solutions to equation: _____   _____

Check: _____

Solution: _____

Name: _____   Date: _____

Quiz IX: Learning About Quadratic Equations

Directions: Complete the following exercises as directed.

Fill in the blanks with the correct word. Select answers from the following list.

factoring	quadratic equation	formula	second degree	c
numbers	completing the square	standard form		

The equation $x^2 + 2x + 4$ is a **1.** _____ _____. It is a quadratic

equation because it is a **2.** _____-_____ polynomial equation. Quadratic

equations may be solved by **3.** _____ and by using the quadratic **4.** _____.

When the quadratic is written as $ax^2 + bx + c = y$, it is in the **5.** _____

_____. In $ax^2 + bx + c = y$ the letters a, b, and c will be replaced by **6.** _____.

In the quadratic equation, the letter **7.** _____ remains constant no matter what value

is given to x.

Rewrite each of the following in standard form.

8. $5x^2 - 2x = 6$ _____

9. $8x^2 + 6x = -4$ _____

Solve the following by factoring.

10. $6x^2 + 4x - 10 = 0$ _____

11. $3x^2 + 19x + 20 = 0$ _____

12. $4x^2 + 5x - 6 = 0$ _____

Solve the following using the quadratic formula.

13. $2x^2 + 3x - 2 = 0$ **14.** $x^2 + 4x + 3 = 0$

Solution: _____   Solution: _____

Answer Keys

Adding Positive and Negative Numbers (p. 1)

1) +6, A
2) -15, A
3) -2, B
4) -68, A
5) +11, B
6) +156, A
7) +3, B
8) -22, B
9) +9, B
10) -143, A
11) +376, A
12) +86, B
13) -11
14) -22
15) -67
16) -129
17) -101
18) -39

Subtracting Positive and Negative Numbers (p. 2)

1) +5, +14
2) -14, -26
3) -18, -107
4) +23, +38
5) +13
6) -35
7) -9
8) difference

Quiz I: Addition and Subtraction With Positive and Negative Numbers (p. 3)

1)   90 (addend)
  + -123 (addend)
    -33 (sum)

2) +79
3) -55
4) +89
5) +99
6) +89
7) -523

8)   90 (minuend)
  - -123 (subtrahend)
    213 (difference)

9) +11
10) -73
11) +159
12) -467

13) +343
14) -455
15) C
16) E
17) D
18) B
19) A

Multiplication with Positive and Negative Numbers (p. 4)

1) +32; like signs rule
2) -480; unlike signs rule
3) -35; unlike signs rule
4) +312; like signs rule
5) 84
6) 360
7) -560
8) -56

Division with Positive and Negative Numbers (p. 5)

1) 6; like signs rule
2) -6; unlike signs rule
3) 6; like signs rule
4) -6; unlike signs rule
5) 128
6) 25
7) -26
8) 56

Quiz II: Multiplication and Division With Positive and Negative Numbers (p. 6)

1) -322
2) 117
3) -5,412
4) 180,900
5) -18,564
6) -246
7) 10
8) -108
9) 1,800
10) -17,820
11) 181,440
12) -6,048
13) will have *positive* sign
14) will have *negative* sign

15) -6
16) 4
17) 8
18) -25
19) 76
20) -48
21) will have the sign of the *negative* number
22) will have *a positive* sign

Variables/Equal, Less Than, Greater Than/ More Mathematical Symbols (p. 8)

1) <
2) >
3) <
4) >
5) <
6) <
7) >
8) >
9) <
10) >
11) =
12) =
13) =
14) >
15) =
16) <

All (numbers 17–20) are *constant* because all letters represent only one possible number value.
17) -12
18) 29
19) 11
20) 4

21–24.   All a) and b) numbers will vary. All c) answers are *variable* because all letters have several possible numeric values.

Math Problems With More Than One Variable (p. 9)

1) (0,6); (-1,7); (-2, 8); (5, 1); (4, 2); (3,3); and vice versa
2) none
3) none
4) (5, 5); (-5, -5)
5) (5, 5); (-5, -5)
6) (2, -1); (1, -2); (0, -3); (3, 0); (4, 1); (5, 2); (6, 3); (7, 4); (8,5)
7) 20
8) 28
9) -28
10) 14
11) 17
12) -7
13) 6
14) -3
15) -8
16) 11
17) -28
18) -21
19) -2
20) 0

Word Problems Using Variables (p. 10)

1) a
2) b
3) $4.50; $10.00
4) a) $4.50; $10.00   b) $4.50; $14.50
   c) $4.50; $12.50   d) $4.50; $8.00
Letter "d" is the correct answer.
5) 2x - 1 = $8.00
6) 2; 4.50; subtract; 1.00
7) teacher check

Quiz III: Mathematical Symbols (p. 11)

1) H
2) J
3) B
4) D
5) A
6) C
7) L
8) F
9) K
10) G
11) E
12) I
13–18) teacher check

Understanding Polynomials (p. 12)

The following numbers should have plus signs in front of them: 2, 4, 5, 6, 7, 8, 10, 12, 13, 14, 17, 19, 21, 23, 24, 28, 30, 32

Terms, Expressions, and Polynomials (p. 13)

The following should have plus signs in front of them: 1, 2, 3, 6, 9, 12, 13, 14, 16, 17, 20

21) B   22) B   23) T   24) T   25) M
26) M   27) M   28) T   29) B   30) M

Adding Polynomials (p. 15)

1) $2x^2$; x^2 2) $7x^3$; x^3 3) y^4; $3y^4$
4) p^4; $2p^4$ 5) t^4; $3t^4$; $10t^4$
6) $4x$; $2x$ 7) $8y^3$; $5y^3$; y^3 and x^3; $2x^3$
8) k; $3k$; $6k$ 9) none
10) $10x^2$; $2x^2$; x^2 11) x
12) $6y$ 13) $3x$ 14) $7x$
15) $4x^2 - 3x + 2y^2$ 16) $2x^2 - 3y^2$
17) $3y^2 - 4x^2$ 18) $2x^4 - x^3 + x^2 + 2y$
19) $2x^4 - x^3 + x^2 + 2y$ 20) $-5x^4 - x^3 + x^2 + y^3$

Subtracting Polynomials (p. 16)

1) $xy - 4x + 4y + 27$ 2) $-5x + b$
3) $x^3 - 3x^2 - 2x + 2y$ 4) $x + 4y - 3a$
5) $12x^3 - x + 11y^2 + 2y$ 6) $11x^3 + 11y^2 + 2y$
7) $-13x^3 - 9y^2$ 8) $-11x^3 - 11y^2 - 2y$

Multiplying Polynomials (p. 17–18)

1) $3x - 3y$ 2) $3x^2 + 3xy$ 3) $t^5 - t^2y^2$
4) $-2x^3 - 2x^2 + 2xy$ 5) $9xy^3$
6) $-15x^4 + 10x^3 - 5x^2y + 5xy$
7) $15x^4 - 10x^3 + 5x^2y - 5xy$
8) $-42x^2y^3$ 9) $42x^3y^3$ 10) $-3a^5$
11) $3x^2 + xy - 2y^2$ 12) $x^3 + x - x^2y - y$
13) $-3x^4 + x^2y^3 + 3x^2y^2 - y^5$ 14) $-x^2 + y^2$
15) $x^2 + xy^3 - y^4 - xy$ 16) $2t^2 - 3x^4t + x^8$

Dividing Polynomials (p. 19–20)

1) x^2 2) y^4 3) t 4) $2x^2$
5) $4y$ 6) x^2 7) x^{-2} or $\frac{1}{x^2}$
8) y^{-4} or $\frac{1}{y^4}$ 9) t^{-1} or $\frac{1}{t}$
10) $-2x^2$ 11) $-4y$ 12) x^2 13) $7x^3 + 3x^2$
14) $y - 1$ 15) $3r^3 - 4r + 2r^{-1}$ or $3r^3 - 4r + \frac{2}{r}$
16) $-7x^3 + -3x^2$ 17) $-y - (-x/y)$ or $-y + \frac{x}{y}$
18) $-7x^3 + 3x^2$ 19) $b + s$ 20) $2c - a$

Quiz IV: Understanding Polynomials (p. 21)

1) D   2) E   3) A   4) B   5) C
6) x^2; $5x^2$ 7) $y^2 + 15y$
8) $8x^2 + 7x - 11y$ 9) $17x^3 + 3y^3 - 6y^2 + 5$
10) $6x^5 + 3x^3y - 4x^2y - 2y^2$ 11) $4y^3 - 2y^2 - y$

Written and Mathematical Expressions (p. 22)

1) $7 + y$ or $y + 7$ 2) $y - 3$
3) $8y$ 4) $5y + 3$
5) $(y/8) + 5$ 6) $5y + 6 = 50$
7) $(y/5) - 7 = 37$ 8) $13y = 117$
9) $5y = 55$ 10) $30 = 2y - 1$

Equations (p. 23)

1) 4   2) 1   3) 5, 8   4) 10, 3
5) 6   6) 6   7) 21, 3   8) 7
9) 4, 8   10) 5

Review of Equation Rules (p. 25–26)

Final answers (part b):
1) 21   2) 12   3) 70   4) 28
5) 7   6) 14   7) 40   8) 10
9) 16   10) 27   11) 64   12) 3,125
13) 60
(part c):
14) 5   15) 64   16) 1   17) 100
18) 14

Learning About Parentheses and Brackets (p. 27–28)

Final answer (part d):
1) 6   2) 1   3) 2   4) 3
5) 5   6) -8   7) 3   8) 2

Order of Operations (p. 29)

Final answer:
1) 2   2) 29   3) -10
4) $5x - 5y - z = x$ 5) $8x = 14a$ 6) $-4.8 = x$

Quiz V: Learning About Equations (p. 30)

1) mathematical statement   2) equality
3) $2x + 1 = 7$ 4) algebraic expressions
5) equal   6) equality   7) added
8) subtracted 9) zero   10) divided
11) left, right   12) parentheses
13) negative 14) positive   15) left, right
16) multiplication, division (any order)
17) addition, subtraction (any order)
18) simplified 19) $x = -1/6$ 20) $2y - 8 = -x$
21) C   22) A   23) B   24) E   25) D

Understanding and Using Exponents (p. 31)

1) 64   2) 27   3) 49   4) 100,000
5) 2,744   6) 16,777,216
7) 19,487,171   8) 40,353,607
9) Five to the third power.

10) Four to the fourth power.
11) Seven to the fifth power.
12) Forty-two to the first power.

Exponents, Bases, and Factors (p. 32)
1) 4   2) 8   3) 16   4) 64
5) 9   6) 27   7) 81   8) 243
9) 16   10) 64   11) 256   12) 1,024
13) 100   14) 1,000
15) 10,000   16) 100,000
17) a) 8^2 b) 64   18) a) 12^8 b) 429,981,696
19) a) 2^6 b) 64   20) a) 4^0 b) 1
21) a) 3^4 b) 81   22) a) 7^1 b) 7

Exponents in Algebraic Expressions (p. 33)
1) 4   2) 27   3) 3,125   4) 28
5) 255   6) 8   7) 12   8) 60
9) 16   10) 48   11) 130   12) 54

13) 52   14) 499   15) $9\frac{1}{25}$

Looking for Patterns When Using Exponents (p. 33)
16) 3   17) 9   18) 27   19) 81   20) c
21) all equal 1   22) a) 8; b) 4; c) 2; d) 1
23) b

Dealing With Negative Exponents and Negative Bases (p. 34)
Final answer:

1) $\frac{1}{4}$ 2) $\frac{1}{81}$ 3) $\frac{1}{64}$ 4) $\frac{1}{216}$

5) $\frac{1}{125}$ 6) $\frac{1}{100}$ 7) 9   8) -243
9) 27   10) -64   11) 125   12) -512
13) -512   14) 25   15) 16

Adding, Subtracting, and Multiplying Exponents (p. 35–36)
1) a) 5^{2+1}; b) 5^3; c) 125
2) a) 6^{3+2}; b) 6^5; c) 7,776
3) a) 7^{3+5}; b) 7^8; c) 5,764,801
4) a) x^{3+2}; b) x^5
5) a) y^{1+4}; b) y^5
6) a) r^{4+2}; b) r^6
7) a) $2^{2 \cdot 3}$; b) 2^6; c) 64
8) a) $2^{4 \cdot 2}$; b) 2^8; c) 256
9) a) $10^{3 \cdot 2}$; b) 10^6; c) 1,000,000
10) a) $7^{1 \cdot 5}$; b) 7^5; c) 16,807
11) a) $5^{3 \cdot 3}$; b) 5^9; c) 1,953,125
12) a) $12^{2 \cdot 2}$; b) 12^4; c) 20,736
13) a) $3^{3 \cdot 4}$; b) 3^{12}; c) 531,441

14) a) $2^{5 \cdot 2}$; b) 2^{10}; c) 1,024
15) a) $3^{2 \cdot 2}$; b) 3^4; c) 81
16) a) $6^{1 \cdot 3}$; b) 6^3; c) 216
17) a) $6^{4 \cdot 2}$; b) 6^2; c) 36
18) a) $7^{5 \cdot 4}$; b) 7^1; c) 7
19) a) $2^{6 \cdot 3}$; b) 2^3; c) 8

20) a) $4^{2 \cdot 5}$; b) 4^{-3}; c) $1/4^3$; d) $\frac{1}{64}$

21) a) $3^{1 \cdot 6}$; b) 3^{-5}; c) $1/3^5$; d) $\frac{1}{243}$
22) a) $x^{4 \cdot 2}$; b) x^2
23) a) $y^{6 \cdot 3}$; b) y^3
24) a) $x^{4 \cdot 6}$; b) x^{-2}; c) $1/x^2$
25) a) $y^{7 \cdot 8}$; b) y^{-1}; c) $1/y$

Quiz VI: Understanding and Using Exponents (p. 37)
1) Four to the sixth power.
2) Three to the fifth power.
3) Two to the fourth power.
4) a) 3; b) 5, 5, 5
5) a) 5; b) 10, 10, 10, 10, 10
6) a) 6; b) 3, 3, 3, 3, 3, 3
7) a) 4; b) y, y, y, y
8) 125   9) 1   10) 10,000
11) 64   12) 64   13) 16   14) 1
15) 125   16) 12   17) 270   18) 96

19) $\frac{1}{4}$ 20) $\frac{1}{3}$ 21) $\frac{1}{25}$

22) 625; 125; 25; 5; 1; $\frac{1}{5}$; $\frac{1}{25}$; $\frac{1}{125}$; $\frac{1}{625}$
23) b   24) d   25) 4,782,969
26) 161,051   27) 390,625

28) 117,649   29) 4,096   30) $\frac{1}{4096}$

Number of Factors (p. 39)
1) a) 3; b) $3 \cdot 3 \cdot 3 \cdot 3$ 2) a) 5; b) $5 \cdot 5 \cdot 5$
3) a) 4; b) $4 \cdot 4 \cdot 4 \cdot 4$
4) a) 4; b) $4 \cdot 4 \cdot 4 \cdot 4 \cdot 4$ 5) a) 3; b) $3 \cdot 3$
6) a) 1.414213562...; b) irrational; c) 2
7) a) 1.732050808...; b) irrational; c) 2
8) a) 1.903653939...; b) irrational; c) 5
9) a) 2; b) rational; c) 3
10) a) 6.164414003...; b) irrational; c) 2

Adding and Subtracting Radicals (p. 40)
Final answer:

1) $3\sqrt{5}$ 2) $6\sqrt{13}$ 3) $15\sqrt{156}$
4) $5\sqrt{2}$ 5) $1\sqrt{7}$ 6) $8\sqrt{8}$

7) 0 or $0\sqrt{12}$ 8) $1\sqrt{10}$
9) $7\sqrt{10}$ 10) $2\sqrt{3}$

Multiplying and Dividing Radicals (p. 41)

1) a) $\sqrt{16}$; b) 4; c) rational
2) a) $\sqrt{16}$; b) 4; c) rational
3) a) $9\sqrt{125}$; b) 100.623059...; c) irrational
4) a) $8\sqrt{xyz}$
5) a) $64\sqrt{48}$; b) 443.4050067...; c) irrational
6) a) $8\sqrt[3]{16}$; b) 20.1587368...; c) irrational
7) a) $\frac{18}{2}$; b) $\sqrt{9}$; c) 3; d) rational
8) a) $\frac{48}{2}$; b) $\sqrt{24}$; c) 4.898979486...;
   d) irrational
9) a) $\frac{16}{4}$; b) $\sqrt{4}$; c) 2; d) rational
10) a) $\frac{125}{5}$; b) $\sqrt[3]{25}$; c) 2.924017738...;
    d) irrational
11) a) $\frac{64}{2}$; b) $\sqrt[5]{32}$; c) 2; d) rational
12) a) x/y; b) $\sqrt[3]{x/y}$

Prime Factors and Simplifying Square Root Radicals (p. 42)

1) 2, 7   2) 2, 3, 5, 2, 5, 2
3) 2, 2, 2, 2, 2, 2, 2, 2, 2   4) 2, 7, 17
5) a) 2, 2, 3; b) $2\sqrt{3}$; c) 3, 3, 2; d) $3\sqrt{2}$;
   e) $2\sqrt{3} + 3\sqrt{2} = 7.706742302...$

Rationalizing the Denominators in Radicals With Fractions (p. 43)

1) $\frac{2\sqrt{5}}{5}$ 2) $\frac{\sqrt{6}}{3}$ 3) $\frac{\sqrt{2}}{2}$
4) 5   5) 2

Learning About Radicals in Equations (p. 44)

Final answers (c):
1) $x = 9$ 2) $x = 16$ 3) $x = 81$
4) $x = 25$ 5) $x = 36$ 6) $x = 49$
7) $x = 64$ 8) $x = 144$ 9) $x = 225$
10) $x = 100$

Quiz VII: Learning About Radicals and Roots (p. 45)

1) $\sqrt{49}$ 2) $\sqrt[4]{64}$ 3) $\sqrt[3]{125}$
4) $\sqrt[8]{256}$ 5) square root of eight
6) cube root of eight
7) sixth root of seventy-eight

8) a) 9; b) 9 • 9   9) a) 2; b) 2 • 2 • 2 • 2
10) a) 3; b) 3 • 3 • 3
11) a) 2; b) 2 • 2 • 2 • 2 • 2
12) $\sqrt{14}$ 13) $\sqrt{35}$ 14) $2\sqrt{18}$
15) $\sqrt{3}$ 16) $\sqrt{3}$ 17) $\sqrt{7}$
18) $2\sqrt{3}$ 19) $15\sqrt{2}$
20) $\frac{\sqrt{3}}{2}$ 21) $\frac{\sqrt{6}}{3}$
22) indexes, radicands
23) because both are square roots and both have radicands of twelve
24) indexes, radicands
25) both are square roots, but the radicands are different

Learning About Linear Equations (p. 46)

First degree equations are: 2, 3, 5, 6, 7
11) $y = 12$ 12) $y = -11$
13) $x = 4$ 14) $x = 6$

Determining the Slope of a Graphed Linear Equation (p. 47–49)

1) straight   2) first   3) linear
4) x; y; 0; 0   5) up; right; positive
6) up; left; positive 7) down; left; negative

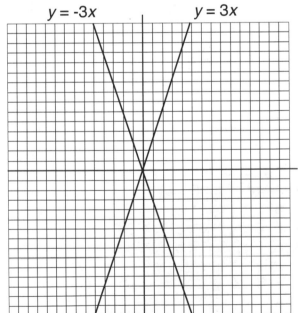

8) $y = 3x$; When read left to right, it slopes upward.
9) $y = -3x$; When read left to right, it slopes downward.

Positive and Negative Slope (p. 50)

1) b 2) up 3) positive 4) a
5) c 6) a 7) c 8) a
9) a 10) c 11) a 12) b

Formula for Determining the Slope of a Graphed Linear Equation (p. 51)

1) Letters a, c, d, e, and f should be marked.
2) teacher check

Graphing Linear Equations and Determining Their Slopes (p. 52–53)

1–3) teacher check

 $y = -2x + 1$  $y = 2x + 1$ $y = 2x - 1$

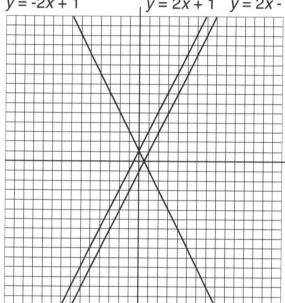

4) positive   5–6) teacher check
7) 2   8) positive
9–10) teacher check   11) 2
12) negative   13–14) teacher check
15) -2

Learning About the x-Intercept and the y-Intercept (p. 54–55)

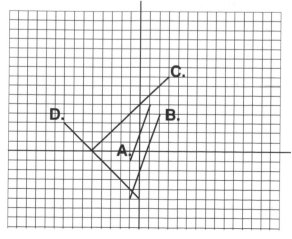

1) A, B, C   2) D   3) 0,2
4) 0,2   5) $-\frac{2}{3}$,0   6) $-\frac{2}{3}$,0
7) $\frac{2}{3}$,0   8) 0,-2   9) -5,0
10) 0,5   11) -5,0   12) 0,-5
13) c   14) c   15) 0; -4
16) x; 1   17) 0; 2   18) x; -2
19) 0   20) 0

Learning About the Slope-Intercept Equation (p. 56–57)

1–4) teacher check 5) c   6) a   7) a
8–11) teacher check   12) a   13) c
14) c   15–18) teacher check   19) d
20) b   21) d   22) $\frac{3}{1}$; 3 23) 3   24) -8

Slope-Intercept Exercises (p. 58)

1) $y = 2x + 1$ 2) $y = 2x + 8$ 3) $y = x + 7$
4) $y = (x + 2)/3$ 5) a) $\frac{4}{1}$; b) 5
6) a) $\frac{1}{2}$; b) -2 7) a) $\frac{1}{1}$; b) 1 8) a) $\frac{1}{1}$; b) 1
9) true   10) true   11) false
12) false   13) d   14) positive

Graphing Linear Equations (p. 59)

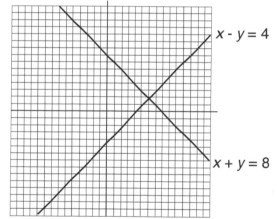

1) b   2) a) 6 + 2 = 8   b) 6 - 2 = 4
3) a) 6,2   b) $x + y = 8$ c) $x - y = 4$

Quiz VIII: Learning About Linear Equations (p. 60)

1) linear equation 2) one   3) positive
4) negative   5) up   6) down
7) $y = -2x + 4$ 8) negative
9) $y = 2x + 4$ 10) positive
11) $y = mx + b$ 12) m   13) b
14) vertical   15) horizontal
16) numerator   17) denominator
18) 10   19) 2

Learning About Quadratic Equations (p. 61)

1) $x^5 + x^3 + x^2 - y$
2) $a^4 + a^3 - a^2$
3) $-4y^4 + 5xy^3 + y^2 - 2$
4) $b^4 - b^3 + 5b^2 + 10b$
5) $x^2 + x - y$
6) $-t^4 + t^3x^2 + 7t^2y^5 + a^3t$
7) $4y^5q^8 + q^3x^2 + 9q$
8) $d^9g^4 + 6d^2r - 2d$
9) $r^8x + 3r^5t - 2a^4r^2 - 4ar$
10) $-8y^3b^2 + y^2x^4 + 6yt^2 + 2y$

Graphing the Equation $ax^2 + bx + c$ (p. 62–63)

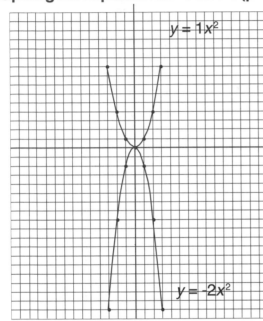

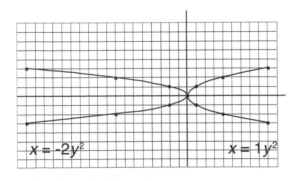

Parabolas (p. 64–65)

1) 1,0   2) decreasing   3) -1,0
4) increasing   5) 1,0   6) decreasing
7) 1,0   8) decreasing   9) maximum
10) minimum   11) vertex   12) -1,0
13) increasing   14) -1,0 15) increasing
16) -1,0 17) increasing   18) 1,0
19) decreasing   20) maximum
21) minimum   22) vertex

Parabola Practice (p. 66)

1) a   2) teacher check   3) a
4) a   5) teacher check   6) b
7) b   8) a   9) teacher check
10) teacher check 11) true 12) y
13) two halves that are mirror images
14) symmectric   15) parabola
16) $y = ax^2$ 17) $y = -2x^2$ 18) 0,0

Solving Quadratic Equations (p. 67)

Final answers are:
1) 11   2) -11   3) -17   4) -9
5) -9   6) 1   7) $x^2 + 8x + 16 = 0$
8) $x^2 - 7x + 6 = 0$ 9) $4x^2 - 16x - 20 = 0$
10) $10x^2 + 6x - 2 = 0$
11) $11x^2 + 3x + 4 = 0$

Solving Quadratics by Factoring (p. 68)

1) a) $(x + 6)(x - 2)$; b) $x = -6$ or $x = 2$
2) a) $(x - 3)(x - 3)$; b) $x = 3$
3) a) $(x + 2)(x + 3)$; b) $x = -2$ or $x = -3$
4) a) $(x - 6)(x - 4)$; b) $x = 6$ or $x = 4$
5) a) $(x - 4)(x - 3)$; b) $x = 4$ or $x = 3$
6) a) $(x + 4)(x + 4)$; b) $x = -4$
7) a) $(x - 1)(x - 1)$; b) $x = 1$
8) a) $(x - 5)(x - 2)$; b) $x = 5$ or $x = 2$
9) a) $(x + 2)(x + 1)$; b) $x = -2$ or $x = -1$
10) a) $(y + 3)(y - 1)$; b) $y = -3$ or $y = 1$

Solving Quadratics by the Quadratic Formula (p. 69–70)

Final answers are:
1) 2, -8   2) 4, -2
3) 3.236…, -1.236…   4) 0.414…,-2.414…
5) 1.35…, -1.85…

Quiz IX: Learning About Quadratic Equations (p. 71)

1) quadratic equation   2) second-degree
3) factoring   4) formula
5) standard form   6) numbers
7) c   8) $5x^2 - 2x - 6 = 0$
9) $8x^2 + 6x + 4 = 0$ 10) $(3x + 5)(2x - 2)$
11) $(3x + 4)(x + 5)$ 12) $(4x - 3)(x + 2)$
13) $-2, \frac{1}{2}$ 14) -3, -1